OBEDIENTIA CIVIUM URBIS FELICITAS

THE MANSION HOUSE
DUBLIN

300 years of history and hospitality

Edited by Mary Clark

First published 2015 by
Dublin City Council
Dublin City Library & Archive
138-144 Pearse Street
Dublin 2
Ireland
Text © The Contributors, 2015

Distributed by
Four Courts Press
7 Malpas Street
Dublin 8
Ireland

A catalogue record for this book is available
from the British Library

ISBN 978-1-907002-19-9 (Case-bound)
ISBN 978-1-907002-20-5

Designed by VERMILLON
Indexed by Julitta Clancy

Previous page: Dining room silverwear bearing
the Lord Mayor's Arms (Conor McCabe)

THE
MANSION HOUSE
DUBLIN

300 years of history and hospitality

Baile Átha Cliath
Dublin City

Decade of Commemorations

1715 2015

TEACH AN ARDMHÉARA
THE MANSION HOUSE

CONTENTS

INTRODUCTION

Ardmhéara Atha Cliath, Críona Ní Dhálaigh

I am honoured to be the 346th Lord Mayor of Dublin and to have the opportunity to reside in this historic building, The Mansion House, during its 300th anniversary as the official residence of the Lord Mayor.

The Mansion House is a building of distinction. It is the oldest free-standing house in Dublin, it is a rare example of Queen Anne style architecture in Dublin, it is the only remaining mayoral residence in Ireland and it is older than any surviving mayoral residence in Britain.

Constructed in 1710 by property developer Joshua Dawson to be his town house, it was obtained by the then Dublin Corporation for use as the official residence of the Lord Mayor. On 18 May 1715, the Corporation purchased the house at a cost of £3,500 sterling and also agreed to pay a yearly rent to Dawson of forty shillings (later waived) and a loaf of double-refined sugar weighing six pounds each Christmas. In return, Joshua Dawson agreed to build on an extra room to the house which could be used for civic receptions - the famous Oak Room. The Oak Room continues to fulfil this function to this day and welcomes thousands of Dubliners, Irish and international visitors yearly.

The Mansion House has been the centre of Dublin's civic life for nearly three hundred years. During the 18th century, the annual City Ball was held in the Oak Room and the Lord Mayor dispensed generous hospitality, aided by a yearly grant of twenty thousand oysters from the civic oyster beds. In 1821, the Round Room was built beside the Mansion House for the visit of King George IV to Dublin and it was constructed in just six weeks. It has since seen many historic events, such as the first meeting of the First Dáil, held in the Round Room on 21 January 1919. In 1864, the original Supper Room was built to afford additional space for civic events; the current building, dating from the 1890s, is the third on this site. In recent years, the Round Room and Supper Room have hosted a range of public activities, ranging from Sales of Work and Antiques Fairs to Irish dancing competitions. Now, the Round Room and Supper Room have a new incarnation as a restaurant and banqueting hall.

As Lord Mayor of Dublin, I am honoured to continue the tradition of welcoming visitors to the Mansion House. It is a unique privilege to live in this wonderful house and attend the many functions which happen within its walls, from local events to civic receptions and the conferring of the Honorary Freedom of the City of Dublin. I am confident that the Mansion House will continue its long tradition of hospitality for many years to come and in due course may it celebrate another three hundred years.

THE MANSION HOUSE, DUBLIN: A BRIEF HISTORY

Mary Clark

Dublin's Mansion House is remarkable for many reasons. Firstly, it is the only mayoral residence in Ireland which is still used to house the Lord Mayor. Secondly, it is earlier than any surviving mayoral residence in England, giving it a unique importance in the civic iconography of Ireland and Britain. Thirdly, it is the oldest free-standing residence in Dublin, with associated architectural and historic significance.[1] Fourthly, it has a hallowed place in Ireland's national history, as the location of the First Dáil, which met in the Mansion House Round Room in 1919. And finally, it has been the centre of the city's hospitality since 1715 and as a result it has established itself in the affections of generations of Dubliners. Additionally, its history mirrors that of the city and country, and according as every political and social change has occurred, the Mansion House has adapted to encompass it.

The creation of an entirely new type of civic building in England and Ireland during the period 1690–1783 added lustre and distinction to emerging Georgian cities. This innovation was the dedicated mayoral residence, which eventually came to be known as the Mansion House, and was introduced to enhance the dignity of the first citizen, who until then had been expected to host civic functions in his own home or in rented accommodation. During this period, seven cities provided Mansion Houses, of which four original buildings have survived and are still used as mayoral residences. The first Mansion House was opened at Newcastle-upon-Tyne in 1691. Built at a cost of £6,000 sterling this was constructed at a time of great prosperity for Newcastle, which also expressed its civic pride by providing its Mayor with a state coach and a gilded barge, as well as an official residence. But by 1837, the cost of funding these trappings of office had become prohibitive for Newcastle-upon-Tyne, and England's first Mansion House was sold to timber merchants, while its contents were auctioned off, and the building was finally destroyed by fire in 1895.[2] Much less wealthy than Newcastle, Dublin purchased a modest Queen Anne house in 1715 from property developer Joshua Dawson, and this has been the mayoral residence ever since, as will be discussed below. York's handsome purpose-built Mansion House, attributed to architect William Etty, was completed in 1730 and remains the official residence of the city's Lord Mayors.[3] Not to be outdone, nearby Doncaster built its Mansion House between 1744 and 1748, to the designs of

Sir Daniel Bellingham, first
Lord Mayor of Dublin:
The 350th anniversary of his
election occurs in 2015
(Dublin Civic Portrait Collection)

James Paine, but curiously the city's Mayor has never lived there, using the building instead for offices and entertainment.[4] London was the fourth English city to construct a mayoral residence. The project was first discussed after the Great Fire of 1666, and in the meantime the city's Lord Mayors lived in temporary accommodation. However, a committee was not set up to build London's mayoral residence until 1735, spurred partly by envy of the residences at Dublin and York.[5] Designed by George Dance the Elder, construction of London's Mansion House began in 1738 and was completed in 1752.[6] Cork was the second city in Ireland to provide a mayoral residence. Designed by Davis Ducart, and built between 1764 and 1767, this building was Italian in style, with Venetian windows, a small Doric entrance and internal stucco work by a student of the Lafrancini brothers. Its role as Cork's Mansion House was short-lived: the building became a seminary in 1842 and has been part of the Mercy Hospital since 1857. Bristol was the fifth English city to acquire a mayoral residence, when an existing building in Queen Square was bought for the Mansion House in 1783, but this was destroyed during the city's notorious riots of 1831.[7]

So Dublin was the second British city to provide a mayoral residence, following the lead of Newcastle-upon-Tyne. Why was this decision taken? The catalyst appears to have been the provision of hospitality, which has long been a primary function of the Dublin mayoralty. Writing in the 16th century, the historian Richard Stanihurst noted that the large sum of £500 was the minimum amount expended on entertainment from his personal fortune by each Mayor of Dublin during his term of office. Patrick Sarsfield, Mayor in 1554–5 and ancestor of his namesake who fought at the Battle of the Boyne, was especially renowned for his generosity. Because the Mayor was not provided with an official residence he was expected to entertain in his own house, and Sarsfield's home was open to all comers from five in the morning until ten at night. During his year of office, Sarsfield's guests consumed twenty tuns of claret, in addition to sack, malmsey, muscadel and other wines, all at the Mayor's personal expense.[8] A tun was a measure of wine, consisting of two pipes: each pipe contained 105 imperial gallons, so twenty tuns of claret represented 4,200 gallons, a generous provision by any standard. And this was in addition to the other wines served at Sarsfield's table! Sack was a dry white Spanish wine popular during the 16th century; malmsey was a fortified red wine; and muscadel was a sweet rich wine, which was often served with desserts. But not every Mayor could afford to be so generous, and in January 1559 the former Mayor, John Spensfield, was re-imbursed by the Dublin City Assembly for the 'drinkings' which he hosted in the Tholsel, or City Hall,[9] while at Michaelmas 1605 the Assembly gave £100 to Mayor John Brice, who had 'suffered great losses by the recent devaluation of copper coin'.[10] Traditionally, the Mayor was expected to entertain the Crown's representative, the Lord Deputy (later known as the Lord Lieutenant) both on his arrival in Dublin and on other occasions afterwards. In 1569, the Mayor of Dublin Walter Cusack, along with the twenty-four Aldermen, welcomed Lord Deputy Sir Henry Sidney on his return to the city following a successful campaign against the Fitzgeralds of Desmond.[11] Preposterously, when the new Lord Lieutenant, Robert Devereux, Earl of Essex, landed in Dublin on 15 April 1599, the Dublin City Assembly passed a motion that he and his retinue of noblemen

O Sydney worthy of tryple re-
nowne,
For plagyng the traytours that
troubled the crowne. 1581.

The Mayor of Dublin, Walter Cusack, and
Aldermen of Dublin welcome
Lord Deputy Sir Henry Sidney on his return
to the city in 1569
(John Derricke, *The Image of Ireland*,
engraving published 1581)

and knights should be entertained at the private house of Mayor James Bellew and to add injury to insult the Assembly offered the Mayor the paltry sum of £20 to assist with the purchase of victuals.[12]

In 1665, the office was raised to the status of Lord Mayor of Dublin, by virtue of implementing a charter issued by Charles I in 1641 which had been in abeyance during the successive war and commonwealth. This charter stated that the title was elevated for 'the greater honour of the city of Dublin, which is the principal place of residence of the [Lord] Deputy and officers of state, and in which are the courts of justice.'[13] The 1660 Restoration of Charles II had been actively supported by Thomas Deey, Mayor of Dublin and the new king was determined to reward the office in an appropriate manner. He granted to the Mayor the right to have a cap of maintenance and a collar of SS; the command of a company of foot soldiers; and an annuity of £500 from the Irish Exchequer.[14] This culminated with authorisation of the title of Lord Mayor. The first incumbent, Sir Daniel Bellingham, took office at Michaelmas 1665 and was determined to surpass all his predecessors. To this end, he built a large residence for himself across the old entrance to Cow Lane, at the corner of Fishamble Street and Castle Street so that he could entertain on a lavish scale.[15] However, Bellingham was a wealthy goldsmith and not every Lord Mayor could afford a house of the requisite size and splendour, fit for civic entertainments.

The question of providing an official residence for the Lord Mayor of Dublin was hotly debated from the beginning of the 18th century. Most men elected to the post were obliged to rent a house large enough to entertain 'the government and persons of quality' since their own homes were too small for this purpose. For the unveiling of King William's statue on 1 July 1701, 'a large new house' was taken on College Green by the Lord Mayor, Sir Mark Rainsford, so that the Lord Justices could be received there. As early as 1702, the City Assembly received a petition requesting that 'a convenient house might be ordered and provided at the expense of the city, for the Lord Mayors of the city.' Instead, a sum of £100 was provided for the Lord Mayor by the city as a rent allowance[16] but this was not always spent wisely. When the 2nd duke of Ormond arrived in Dublin as Lord Lieutenant on 12 August 1703, the Lord Mayor, Thomas Bell, received him not in a house but in a tent on St. Stephen's Green, where Ormond was entertained for an hour, before he proceeded to the Tholsel, Dublin's City Hall.[17] In the previous year, the Lord Mayor elect, Alderman Loyd, had taken a lease from John Hansard of a substantial house on Lazy Hill and commissioned him to fit it out so that it would be suitable for Loyd to use during his term of office. However, Loyd later decided not to serve as Lord Mayor and he refused to pay Hansard the sum of £400 which he owed the builder for his work on the house. When the City Assembly finally discovered this, it felt obliged to pay Hansard £40 sterling as a gesture of compensation, a sum which allowed him and his family to emigrate to New York.[18] This debacle emphasised that an official mayoral residence was now essential for Dublin, if only to prevent further embarrassment.

In 1712, the Dublin City Assembly set up a committee which examined three options: Colonel Allen's house, Joseph Leeson's house on the north side of St. Stephen's Green, and Lord Longford's house in Aungier Street.[19] The location of Colonel Allen's house is not documented,[20] while the house belonging to brewer Joseph Leeson was on the site of the present Kildare Street and University Club at 17 St. Stephen's Green.[21] Lord Longford's house was the preferred option. It could be acquired for £650 sterling and then demolished, so that the site could be used to build the intended mayoral residence in Aungier Street. It was decided to proceed with the Longford house, subject to provision of 'a good and legal title.' At Easter 1713, the committee reported that the agreement between the city and Lord Longford had been settled but was 'obstructed for want of some letters, which are suddenly expected from England' so that it could not be sealed.[22] No more is heard of this agreement or of the Aungier Street site, which suggests either that the letters failed to arrive or else when they did they contravened Longford's title. The matter rested there until Easter 1714, when Joshua Dawson offered the city a choice of two properties which he owned, either of which might be adapted for the Lord Mayor's house.

Born in 1660, Joshua Dawson was a member of the guild of merchants who was admitted to the freedom of Dublin at Christmas 1702. His family came from Dawson's Bridge in Co. Derry and he later helped to develop the village of Castledawson in the same location. As his older brother Thomas was heir to the family estates, Joshua moved to Dublin to further his career. A civil servant by profession, and also M.P. for the Borough of Wicklow, Dawson was based in Dublin Castle as chief secretary to the Lord Justices of Ireland, and according to recent research, Dawson maintained a network of spies who were dedicated to the removal of Catholic priests from Ireland.[23] He was also well placed to identify trends in the development of the city and was among the first to realise that Dublin had the potential to expand eastwards of its medieval core.

Joshua Dawson painted in 1711, when he
was Secretary in Dublin Castle and M.P. for
Borough of Wicklow (Courtesy Lady Moyola)

Thomas Dawson sold the family estates to his brother Joshua, and this new
acquisition spurred him on to make his fortune in Dublin, with a view to restoring
and improving his patrimony. In 1705 Dawson purchased a tract of land to the
east of Grafton Street from Henry Temple, which was described as a piece of
marshy land without even a lane crossing it. Two years later, Dawson had drained
the ground and laid out a wide and straight road, parallel to Grafton Street,
naming it Dawson Street in his own honour, and by 1709 he had issued building
leases for the construction of houses along the street. The building and
development of Duke Street and Anne Street followed, linking Dawson Street
with the earlier Grafton Street. The consolidation of this new suburb was assisted
through the creation of St. Ann's Parish by Act of Parliament in 1707, which not
only conferred the benefits of the established church on the area, but also
allowed for the introduction of basic social services, such as fire-fighting, schools,
street lighting and cleaning, along with poor relief, which were all functions of

the parish vestry.[25] It was Dawson who presented the new parish with a substantial site for erecting a church and vicarage house and for enclosing a churchyard and a separate garden for the vicar's use. He also agreed to have four houses pulled down, so that Dawson Street could be linked with the adjoining Molesworth Street, thus improving access to the church. [26] Finally, in 1710 he built a large house as his private family residence in Dawson Street, near to St. Ann's Church.

As we have seen, at Easter 1714 Dawson had offered the Dublin City Assembly a choice of two buildings to become the new mayoral residence. The first was 'a good house' near St. Andrew's Church, just off Dame Street, and the second was his own family residence near St. Stephen's Green.[27] Dawson was anxious to leave Dublin and return to his family estates in Co. Derry; the death of his patron Queen Anne on 1 August 1714 would add impetus to this wish. The City Assembly favoured Dawson's residence, which was available at a cost of £3,500 sterling, a price which met with their approval, subject to certain improvements.[28] Dawson was required to build an additional large room, 33 feet 10 inches long and 25 feet wide and 14 feet high, and to wainscot, paint and finish it completely: this became known as the Oak Room, and it is still used for civic receptions. Along with the house, he assigned stables, outhouses and the garden to the City Assembly. In return, Dawson reserved the right to a yearly rent of forty shillings (which he later waived) and the right to a loaf of double-refined sugar weighing six pounds, every Christmas if demanded.[29] Dawson robustly maintained that the purchase price of £3,500 would leave him out of pocket as the house cost him £3,200 to build; constructing the Oak Room cost him a further £200; the value of the furniture he was leaving cost him £110 and the locks were worth £30 sterling.[30] Nevertheless, Dawson had to wait for his money, as he was obliged to allow the City Assembly to pay him in instalments: he was paid £1,000 on 18 May 1715 and the remaining £2,500 in three equal instalments of £833-6s-8d on 1 May 1716, 1717 and 1718.[31]

The plan attached to the deed outlines the ground obtained by the City Assembly as part of the purchase of Dawson's house. It was quite extensive, comprising 424 feet 6 inches along Dawson Street as far as the King's Street

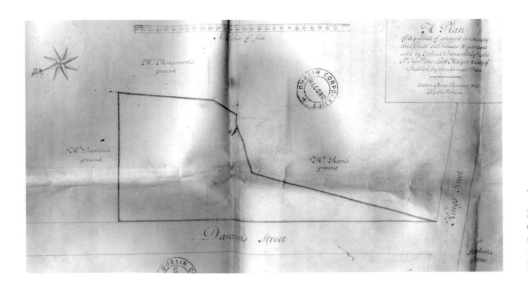

Plan on parchment of Mansion House Ground by Thomas Moland, 1715 From the original deed dated 18 May 1715 (Dublin City Library & Archive, Deeds to the City, No. 13)

(now St. Stephen's Green North); 120 feet to the east adjoining Mr. [Robert] Molesworth's ground; 256 feet 3 inches to the east adjoining Mr. [Abel] Ram's ground; and 86 feet to the south.

Dawson agreed to leave the house and outhouses in good repair with brass locks and marble chimney pieces retained and he gave assurance of a secure, undoubted and uncontested title. He was also required to leave existing furnishings in many of the rooms. These included tapestry hangings, silk curtains and window seats along with a chimney glass in the great bed-chamber, which is still the Lord Mayor's bedroom to this day, although the original furnishings have vanished long ago. The walnut parlour, which is now called the Lady Mayoress' parlour, boasted gilt leather hangings, four pairs of scarlet calamanco window curtains, made of wool with a checked pattern, and a chimney glass. The Danzick oak parlour, which is now part of the drawing room, was furnished with Indian calico curtains and window seats and yet another chimney glass.[32]

At the Midsummer meeting of the City Assembly in July 1715, the purchase committee reported that the Lord Mayor's house was nearly ready. The deeds had been perfected (and the indenture was signed on 18 May 1715);[33] the new room was built, was ready for covering and was to be furnished with tables, chairs and window curtains; the kitchens were to be made fit for the Lord Mayor's use and provided with spits, racks and jacks; and the chaplain's room was to be furnished with bed, chairs and a table.[34] The committee was instructed to continue until the work had been finished. At Midsummer 1716, since there was no further occasion for continuing the committee for the Lord Mayor's

Inventory on parchment of fittings and furnishings left in the Mansion House by Joshua Dawson (From the original deed dated 18 May 1715)

house, it was dissolved, and another committee was appointed to take an inventory of all the city's goods in the Lord Mayor's house, the inventory to be lodged in the Tholsel office.[35]

The honour of being the first Lord Mayor to reside in the new mayoral residence went to John Stoyte, who held office for the civic year 1715-6.[36] Stoyte was a merchant who gained the Dublin franchise at Michaelmas 1699 on completion of an apprenticeship to his brother Francis, another merchant who was remarkably successful. Francis Stoyte is recorded in St. Werburgh's Parish in 1680 and he was living in Cork Hill (within the same parish) in 1694 and 1705. He was Sheriff of Dublin for the civic year 1692-3 and Lord Mayor of Dublin for the civic year 1704-5 and by then he had been knighted and was Sir Francis Stoyte. John Stoyte was Sheriff of Dublin for the civic year 1701-2 and is recorded as living in St. Werburgh Street in 1705-6.[37] His term of office as Lord Mayor 1715-6 was remarkably busy and expensive. On 13 April 1716 he sent a petition to the City Assembly noting that he had been 'at extraordinary expense on his coming into the new [Lord Mayor's] house, as also by reason of a new government in his Lordship's time of Mayoralty, a parliament likewise sitting and the franchises to be rid.'[38] Acknowledging that Stoyte was indeed out of pocket, the City Assembly reimbursed him in the amount of £400 sterling.

Dublin's new mayoral residence underwent many changes of name before finally becoming known as the Mansion House. At first, it was called 'the Lord Mayor's house' and it appears under this title in an engraving published with Charles Brooking's map of Dublin, dated 1728. Here it is shown as a plain but dignified Queen Anne house set in its own wooded grounds, with two storeys surmounted by a frieze inset with life-size male statues, possibly representing mythological figures.[39] These statues have long since vanished, and the original façade now lies hidden under a Victorian exterior, while the woodlands have been largely built over, leaving only a small garden beside the residence. The architect is unknown, but it is likely that Joshua Dawson was in part responsible for the design. His talent as a town planner is evident in the layout of his family village of Castledawson, which he re-designed early in the 18th century.[40] From 1743, the Lord Mayor's House was known as Mayoralty House[41] a term which was also used for the mayoral residence in Cork, when it was built during the 1760s. The family home of the Dalys of Galway, built in 1730, was popularly known as Mayoralty House because several members of this family served the city as Mayor, but it was not an official civic residence.[42] The name Mayoralty House was also applied to a building erected by the corporation of Drogheda in 1765, but this was a venue for civic receptions and not a mayoral residence. In some Irish boroughs, the first citizen was called 'sovereign' rather than Mayor, as in Kinsale and Armagh, which each boasted a Sovereign House. However, these were private houses which were owned by first citizens, and not official residences.[43] Dublin and Cork alone provided mayoral residences in Ireland, and as we have seen only Dublin's remains. When London built its mayoral residence, it was known as the Mansion House, a term which was originally applied to any large house, usually the principal house on an estate. By 1776 Dublin had dropped the term Mayoralty House and replaced this with the London usage. Nowadays, the term Mansion House is reserved for the residence of a Lord Mayor.

The new Lord Mayor's House was well-received. An anonymous 'Citizen of London' who observed it in 1732, commented: 'In Dublin is a palace the Lord Mayors keep their Mayoralty in'[44] and indeed the First Citizen was permitted to entertain in some style at his official residence. He had an annuity of £500 sterling for this purpose along with ten thousand oysters from the civic oyster beds.[45] His domestic comforts were also provided for, as there was a housekeeper in residence and fresh milk available daily from a dairy in the extensive gardens.[46] The Lord Mayor's Ball was the principal highlight of the year. The ball took place in the Oak Room on St. Stephen's night (26 December) and the principal invited guests were the city's twenty-four Aldermen and their wives. It appears to have been a charity ball, with proceeds going towards the support of poor boys at the Blue-Coat School in Blackhall Place. Entertainment was provided by the city musicians, under the direction of Lewis Layfield, who had been an actor on the London stage. Perhaps jealous because they were not invited, the members of the lower house on the Dublin City Assembly, the Commons, successfully managed to have the ball abolished in 1728, on the grounds that it was causing 'great inconveniences' along with riotous behaviour.[47] It was replaced by a more sedate dinner for the Aldermen and their wives, which was hosted by the Lord Mayor and Lady Mayoress. Following the dinner, two loving cups were circulated so that a communal toast could be drunk. The larger Williamson Cup was circulated by the Lord Mayor and the smaller Fownes Cup was circulated by the Lady Mayoress.[48]

Each person at the dinner drank from the cup as a sign of goodwill – the cups were made of silver, which has antiseptic properties, so in theory at least, disease would not be spread.

The first Lord Mayors to live in the residence between 1715 and 1760 were Whigs and were supporters of the new Hanoverian regime in London.[49] They were usually members of the guild of merchants and were elected on seniority, having served in the Dublin City Assembly successively as representatives of their guild; as City Sheriff; as Sheriff's Peer; and as Alderman. They generally served one term which began and ended at Michaelmas. Engravings of four holders of the office during this period attest to the popularity of Dublin's Lord Mayors, suggesting a ready market for such images. These were three-quarter

The Sir William Fownes Standing Cup (*left*) and the Sir Joseph Williamson Standing Cup (Dublin Civic Regalia Collection)

length portraits of Humphrey French, Lord Mayor in 1732–3 (unattributed engraving); of Thomas How, Lord Mayor in 1733–4 (mezzotint by John Brooks); and of Sir Samuel Cooke, Lord Mayor in 1740–1 (by James Latham, engraved in mezzotint by John Faber and published in Dublin by John Brooks); along with a full-length portrait of William Aldrich, Lord Mayor in 1741–2 (by Anthony Lee and engraved in mezzotint by John Brooks). The Lord Mayors depicted in these engravings were well-known to the public for a variety of reasons. French was beloved for his charity to the poor, and his engraving is captioned 'The Good Lord Mayor.' Renowned for his integrity, he was elected M.P. for Dublin City in 1733, with the endorsement of Jonathan Swift, and earned the sobriquet of 'patriot' from his fellow-citizens.[50] French also had an advanced sense of the importance of his mayoral office. At the public ceremonies for the birthday of George II on 30 October 1732, French provided a state coach for himself as Lord Mayor, which was drawn by six horses, and a second coach for his footmen, drawn by two horses.[51] In this, he was well ahead of his time, because nearly sixty years would elapse before the City Assembly provided an official state coach for Dublin's first citizen. Cooke was a successful local brewer who was elected as MP for Dublin city in 1749 and was later honoured with the title of 'patriot' for his opposition to the money bill of 1753, which sought to limit the powers of the Irish parliament.[52] Aldrich was a chandler by trade and in 1719, together with his business partner Hugh Cuming, he secured a contract for supplying the city of Dublin with public lighting, which was confirmed by act of parliament in the following year. The two men undertook to provide lanterns, lamps and iron brackets and to light the streets in the city and liberties on all moonless nights between 1 September and 15 April, from one hour after sunset until 2 a.m.[53] The engravings of Aldrich and How were published in London by T. Jeffreys, at the corner of St. Martin's Lane, Charing Cross and by W. Herbert at the Golden Globe on London Bridge. This brought the image of the Dublin mayoralty to the rival capital for the first time, and attests to the growing importance of the smaller city.

Humphrey French, Lord Mayor of
Dublin 1732-3 (From Calendar of
Ancient Records of Dublin, vol. VII)

By the 1740s Dublin's mayoral residence was suffering from structural problems and the roof had to be re-slated. By 1758, the furnishings were in such poor condition that the City Assembly set up a standing committee, which was allowed to spend up to £100 each year on furniture and repairs to the residence.[54] During the 1760s the disposition of rooms on the ground floor was altered, creating the lay-out which is still evident to this day. A series of small rooms on the north side were combined into one large drawing room while a corresponding series of small rooms on the south side were merged to form the dining room.[55] The creation of these two large rooms allowed suitable space and scale for the introduction of full-length portraits to the residence, the first of which was commissioned in 1765.[56] It is likely that the original wall-hangings provided by Joshua Dawson had either perished by this stage or were no longer considered suitable for these new rooms. Certainly, wall-hangings – which in Dawson's day were perhaps old-fashioned – were by now hopelessly outdated. A painting by James Worsdale, who was active in Ireland from 1735 until his death in 1767, shows a panelled room in an Irish house, similar to the Oak Room in the mayoral residence. Here, however, the room has been hung with full-length portraits, three quarter lengths and busts.[57] It was time to begin furnishing the Lord Mayor's house with works of art in a similar manner. In 1765, the Mansion House acquired its first portrait, of the outgoing Lord Lieutenant, the first Duke of Northumberland. This was commissioned by the Dublin City Assembly from Sir Joshua Reynolds, but was paid for by Northumberland himself. A second viceregal portrait soon followed, of Northumberland's successor, Viscount Townshend, executed by the Dublin artist Thomas Hickey. The two portraits were treated as a pendant pair and were placed in identical Rococo frames, which have been attributed to the Dublin wood-carver Richard Cranfield. For the remainder of the 18th century, the City Assembly continued to commission portraits of Lord Lieutenants for the Mansion House. Sitters were chosen if they supported the Assembly's twin objectives: Free Trade and an independent Parliament for Ireland. This is reflected in the portrait of Townshend. He is shown holding the Octennial Act which he sponsored, and which made it mandatory to hold Irish parliamentary elections every eight years, a small but essential step in the liberalisation of government. Townshend also supported Free Trade and made a point of only wearing clothes that had been made in Ireland. This is reflected in his portrait, where his robes have been arranged so that the sumptuous suit of clothes underneath can be seen clearly.

Grattan's Parliament was established in 1782, and this confirmed Dublin's status as the capital of Ireland and the second city of the Empire. The Dublin City Assembly was at pains to enhance the position of the Lord Mayor and to this end provided a splendid new State Coach by William Whitton of Dublin, which first appeared in the city streets in 1791, accompanied by the new Battle-Axe Guard, a ceremonial group of men carrying halberds. New stables were then built behind the Mansion House to accommodate the coach.

In 1792, in an attempt to underline the importance of Dublin's first citizen, the City Assembly first considered the possibility of building a brand-new Mansion House in the centre of St. Stephen's Green.[58] This proposal was examined in more detail in 1809, at a time when the cost of ongoing repairs to Dawson's building was beginning to escalate. The Assembly calculated that the cost of constructing a new Mansion House would be £20,000 – a sum which would be raised in part by lotteries and in part by demolishing the existing mayoral residence and setting the ground in building lots.[59] The proposed new Mansion House was to be both imposing and majestic. Although architect's plans are not available – and indeed the project may never have got that far – we know that the building was intended to have four facades of equal importance, each one reached by its own dedicated pathway through St. Stephen's Green. In the event, Dawson's historic building was spared. Authorisation for the proposed lotteries was not forthcoming from the Westminster parliament, and a shortfall of £11,000 in the city's accounts, discovered in 1814 and attributed to the City Treasurer,

The State Coach of the Lord Mayor of Dublin
(Photograph by George Munday)

had to be replenished, leaving no spare money for a new Mansion House.[60] Instead, the historic Mansion House received a new lease of life when the City Assembly decided to finance its repair and maintenance from a levy of £400 on newly-elected aldermen.[61]

It is interesting that there was no public outcry at the proposal to replace Dawson's Mansion House with something more modern. After serving the city faithfully for one hundred years, there seemed to be little affection for the building. The Mansion House was not featured in James Malton's *Picturesque and Descriptive View of the City of Dublin,* published between 1792 and 1799 even though another civic building, the Dublin Tholsel, was shown. Later artists and engravers, such as Samuel Brocas and George Petrie, similarly ignored the mayoral residence. Some authors writing about Dublin did make reference to the Mansion House, but they were not always complimentary. Writing in 1821, on the eve of George IV's visit to Dublin, John James McGregor described it as 'a mean brick building, by no means according with the other public edifices of the metropolis.'[62] Writing in 1825, G.N. Wright observed of the Mansion House: 'Its appearance is unprepossessing, being fronted entirely with brick, and built after a design which never could have been pleasing to the eye.'[63]

The state visit to Dublin by George IV in 1821 provided fresh impetus for improving Dublin's Mansion House. Over £600 was spent in repairing the building and the huge sum of £8,000 sterling was raised from the aldermen for an extension to the Mansion House, for the reception of the king. This extension was designed by the noted architect John Semple and took the form of a large circular room, known officially as the King's Room and popularly as the Round Room. [64] This was dominated by a superb portrait of George IV by Sir Thomas Lawrence in a magnificent gilt frame by Thomas Byfeld of London, which was

commissioned by the monarch and presented as a memento of his visit – this portrait is still in the residence and is displayed in the Staircase Hall[65] Sadly, Semple's plans for the Round Room are not known to have survived but ground plans by A.R. Neville dated 1829 show the room as it was built. The royal visit was announced on 18 January 1821 and began on 23 August leaving just seven months to raise the money, commission the design and construct the Round Room, which was built by the Dublin firm of Mountiford John Hay.

The Lord Mayor of Dublin, Sir Abraham Bradley King, welcoming George IV to the City of Dublin, 23 August 1821. (From a print after Joseph Haverty, courtesy Kildare Street and University Club)

The *Freeman's Journal* of 24 August noted that the Round Room 'was intended to resemble the circular court-yard of an Arabian Palace. It is surrounded by a battlemented rampart about 22 feet high.... [and] the ceiling was painted to represent a sky.' Many have marvelled at the speed with which the Round Room was constructed but the secret was simple: it was built with a temporary roof! A permanent roof was not supplied until 1824, again to the design of John Semple, and this remained in place until it was replaced by Dublin City Council in 1999.[66]

During the 1830s, the Dublin City Assembly focused its attention primarily on resisting Daniel O'Connell's campaign for municipal reform, which would admit Roman Catholics to civic government in Ireland. In June 1831, O'Connell rented the Round Room as the venue for a huge Reform Dinner, with over six hundred gentlemen present to support his cause. Meanwhile, the City Assembly's time, money and resources were devoted to retaining their sectarian and oligarchic domination of the city, and the Mansion House was allowed to run down. As a result, when O'Connell's triumph was marked on 1 November 1841 by his election as the first Catholic Lord Mayor of Dublin since 1690, the Mansion House was in such a poor state of repair that he was unable to live there. Temporary repairs were put in place, a gas-supply for lighting was installed in 1845 and the interior was completely refurbished in 1850.[67] The stuccoed west

The Mansion House from Henry Shaw's Dublin Directory 1850

façade, with its balustrades, pediment and moulded window surrounds, dates from the following year, 1851, and is by City Architect Hugh Byrne.[68] A last view of the Mansion House façade, as Joshua Dawson left it, can be seen in Henry Shaw's *Dublin Directory* of the previous year, 1850.[69]

In 1864, the Supper Room was added to host medium-sized public receptions, which were too large for the Oak Room and too small for the Round Room. Again, the design was by City Architect Hugh Byrne. The façade reached its present appearance in 1886 with the addition of a pretty iron porch designed by then City Architect Daniel J. Freeman.[70]

Daniel O'Connell instituted an early form of power-sharing which was called the 'Mayoralty Compact'. This meant that the office of Lord Mayor was rotated between a nationalist one year, and a unionist the next year. This informal arrangement mostly proved to be workable and lasted until 1880, when the franchise was enlarged and the nationalists took decisive control of Dublin City Council. Accordingly, when O'Connell left office in 1842 he was succeeded by the unionist George Roe, on O'Connell's nomination.

John L. Arabin, a supporter of O'Connell and a member of the Church of Ireland, served as Lord Mayor of Dublin for the year 1845. The Great Famine began during his mayoralty and on 21 October 1845 Dublin City Council appointed a Mansion House Committee 'to enquire into and report on the disease of the Potato Crop and report on any course they may consider best to be adopted under the circumstances'. On 10 December 1845, the City Council submitted an address to Queen Victoria referring (in vain) to 'the destitution of our Country' warning her that 'the whole population [are] falling victims of the scourge of famine and pestilence' and urging her 'to call Parliament to be assembled.......[so] that such measures be passed..... [as will] enable Your Majesty to be the saviour of your Irish people'.[71] This committee was one of the first agencies to realize the scale of the Great Famine and the danger which it posed to the people.

From 1850 until 1880 the Mansion House was the centre of a lively social life. The year began with 'Lord Mayor's Day' when the outgoing and incoming Lord Mayors in full pomp with the City Sword-bearer and Mace-bearer accompanied by the Aldermen and Councillors went in a procession of carriages to City Hall for the investiture of the new Lord Mayor. The Lord Mayors tended to be successful and wealthy businessmen, including silk and poplin manufacturer Richard Atkinson; the brewer Benjamin Lee Guinness; and the seed merchant James William Mackey. These Lord Mayors accepted the Act of Union and they were either members of the Liberal Party or the Conservative Party, both of which had their headquarters in London. They regularly attended Viceregal balls and levees at Dublin Castle, and thus attracted the derogatory nickname, 'Castle Catholics'. Each Lord Mayor was provided with a yearly allowance of £1,000 to cover the cost of his year in office but this was raised to £2,000 annually in 1851.

During the 19th century the Lord Mayor took up office on 1 January and this was an occasion for much spectacle, welcome at the gloomiest time of the year. The outgoing Lord Mayor was conveyed from the Mansion House to City Hall, where the incoming Lord Mayor was invested with the chain of office and the procession returned to the mayoral residence. One commentator noted 'the magnificence of the Lord Mayor's Show' and continued: The marvellous work of art known as the gingerbread coach moves in graceful measure through the

Photograph of John L. Arabin, Lord Mayor of Dublin 1845 (Dublin City Library & Archive, Mayoral Photographs)

streets, succeeded by other chariots of a less entrancing description drawn by steeds vastly unromantic. Two military bands and a fire brigade make up the display, brass instruments and brass helmets, French horn and fog horn…In the Council Chamber itself the scene is animated, fur cloaks and cocked hats, the splendid mace, the double row of benches contrived for debate and the gallery filled with a patriotic company. The reception of the new civic monarch is always hearty. Kings are ever popular when crowned whatever happens afterwards…the procession winds back to the Mansion House under the gaslights and a dinner in the evening closes the ceremony.'[72]

The Lord Mayor's Ball was revived in September 1861 for the visit to Dublin of the Prince of Wales and the venue was the Round Room. This proved to be a boon to local businesses, with Mrs. Sidford of 17 Nassau Street advertising 'Ball dresses in Fancy and Light-Coloured Silks' while James Forrest and Sons of

Grafton Street had 'Fancy Tulle and Tarleton Dresses, Sylphide Wreaths and Head-dresses' for consideration. *The Irish Times* praised the House Steward, Mr. McCleaverty, stating that his arrangements for the ball were 'so perfect that although there were over 100 persons present, no inconvenience resulted to the guests'. Advertisements in the same newspaper looking for property lost at the ball told a different story: one lady lost a malachite and silver bracelet and was willing to offer a reward 'if found by a poor person'; while another lost a decorative coin from her Maltese bracelet, as well as an embroidered handkerchief trimmed with Honiton lace. Similar hospitality was laid on for the visit of another of Queen Victoria's sons, the Duke of Edinburgh, when he visited Dublin in 1872. The Round Room was decorated and the Supper Room was papered; curtains were taken down, cleaned and put back; the portraits were also cleaned; pot-plants were hired to give a festive air; a brand-new City Flag was commissioned; a pavilion was erected in the garden; and the City Council's lighting expert William Cotton was recalled urgently from his holiday in Harwich – even his travel expenses were paid![73]

Most Lord Mayors preferred to host a banquet instead of a ball. In 1872, Robert Garde Durdin hosted the Lord Mayor's Banquet in the Mansion House, and it was reported that the Round Room 'was brilliantly lighted and decorated for the occasion……the shrubs staged at regular intervals imparted a light and refreshing appearance to the room. The band of the 5th Fusiliers was stationed [next-door] in the Oak Room, and played a pleasing selection of music during dinner, which was supplied by Messrs. Murray and Walsh. A guard of honour, furnished by the Grenadier Guards, received the Lord Lieutenant and Countess Spencer on their arrival.' [74] In 1881, Lord Mayor Sir George Moyers held a very successful banquet to welcome the Prince of Teck. Some 200 people attended the banquet at which a range of dishes was served. Soup was a choice of Tortue Claire or Turtle Punch,

Ball given at the Mansion House for the visit of the Prince of Wales, 1861 (From *The Illustrated London News*)

accompanied by sherry. There were two fish dishes on offer, turbot or sole with white wine. The entrees included *vol-aux-vents, ris de veau aux truffes* and mutton cutlets, all served with champagne. Dessert was *Glace Napolitaine* served with curacao and cognac followed by a choice of fruit with Bordeaux. An end-of-term ball was also hosted by Moyers at the Mansion House on 8 December, with 800 guests invited and music supplied by the band of the 47th Regiment. Such hospitality was necessarily expensive but Moyers benefited by a further increase in the Lord Mayor's salary, from £2,000 to £3,000 (with an additional allowance of £262 for his secretary) which was voted through by Dublin City Council on 15 August 1881, despite a public petition signed by 300 leading citizens objecting to this, on the grounds that the city could not afford it. However, the Council was persuaded that the new arrangement would enable persons to take the office who were not independently wealthy.

Changes to the municipal franchise in 1880 gave Dublin City Council a more nationalist composition. Most of the Lord Mayors during that decade were members of Charles Stewart Parnell's Home Rule Party and many of them had an acute social conscience. Life at the Mansion House now became much more serious. Edmund Dwyer Gray, who was Lord Mayor in 1880, championed the cause of the Irish tenant-farmers, many of whom were suffering from hunger and want because of successive harvest failures in the late 1870s, an event which was known as the Little Famine. Dwyer Gray set up the Mansion House Fund for Relief of Distress in Ireland and used the *Freeman's Journal,* of which he was editor, to lobby for financial contributions, which were then used to purchase food for distribution through more than 800 local committees throughout the 32 counties of Ireland. He was also entrusted with 100,000 dollars voted by the dominion government of Canada to relieve hardship caused by the Little Famine and he used this fund to help provide fishing boats and safe harbours – the idea being that if the harvest on land failed there would be an alternative harvest available by sea.[75] Plaques in the Mansion House entrance hall commemorate these funds and their impact on Ireland. Another Home Rule Lord Mayor was William Meagher, who was M.P. for Co. Meath.

Other Parnellite Lord Mayors were also active in support of their leader's policies. Timothy Daniel Sullivan was an M.P. representing the College Green Division of Dublin City and was a member of Charles Stewart Parnell's Home Rule Party. Elected Lord Mayor of Dublin in 1887, on 2 December that year, Sullivan was imprisoned in Tullamore Jail, Co. Offaly because of his support for the outlawed Plan of Campaign. The scheme, which was initiated by the Land League, advised tenants to combine together to offer their landlords a fair but reduced rent. If the landlord refused to accept this, the tenants were to pay him nothing, but instead were to pay their rents into a 'fighting fund' to sustain any tenants who were evicted. To show their support for their imprisoned Lord Mayor, Dublin City Council voted unanimously on 10 December 1887 to grant the Freedom of the City to T.D. Sullivan. Another staunch supporter was Thomas Sexton, who was Lord Mayor of Dublin in 1888 and 1889. In October 1881, when Parnell was arrested for his opposition to the Irish Land Act, Sexton was imprisoned alongside him in Kilmainham Jail. The division in the Home Rule Party triggered by Parnell's involvement with Mrs. O'Shea led to acrimony on Dublin City Council but his untimely death in October 1891 brought the factions

Alderman William Meagher, M.P.
Lord Mayor of Dublin 1884
Photograph by Lafayette

together at least on a temporary basis and the Council offered City Hall for the lying-in-state of the lost leader. It also commissioned a posthumous portrait of Parnell from the society artist Sir Thomas Alfred Jones which is on display in the Oak Room.

A number of Lord Mayors from the 1890s and 1900s are featured in James Joyce's *Ulysses*, where the action takes place on 16 June 1904. These included Valentine Blake Dillon (1894–5); Daniel Tallon (1897–9); Joseph Hutchinson (1904–06); Timothy C. Harrington (1901–03) and J.P. Nannetti (1906–08). Val Dillon attended the annual dinner at Glencree Reformatory which was a boiled shirt affair. [76] The Council Chamber was in uproar because Hutchinson was in Llandudno and little Lorcan Sherlock was doing *locum tenens* for him.[77] Late Lord Mayor Harrington was in scarlet robe with mace and gold mayoral chain.[78] There were also references to the Lord Mayor's 'gingerbread coach.'[79] The protagonist Bloom even fantasises about achieving mayoral office when he hears chimes and says to himself 'Turn again Leopold, Lord Mayor of Dublin.'[80] The most notorious Lord Mayor from those decades, Joseph Michael Meade, is not mentioned in *Ulysses*. He was a successful and wealthy builder who purchased several large houses in Henrietta Street and partitioned them to become tenements which quickly degenerated into slums. His activities, and those of other aldermen who were slum landlords, were very much at variance with efforts by Dublin City Council to build 'Housing for the Working Class' from 1890 onwards.

The census returns for 1901 and 1911 help to give a picture of the Mansion House as a family home. The nationalist Timothy C. Harrington, originally from Co. Cork, was Lord Mayor in 1901 and the census was taken on 31 March that year. He lived in the Mansion House with his wife Elizabeth and their five children, Eileen (aged 6), Moira (5), Brendan (3), Oona (1) and baby Niall. The Lady Mayoress' mother Elizabeth O'Neill was also present on Census Night and may be supposed to have lived with the family. The housekeeper was Julia Fagan and she had six servants to assist her. James Cooney from Co. Meath was the butler; Mary Kiernan from Co. Meath was the cook; Rose Carey was the governess; Elizabeth Clery from Co. Wicklow was a nurse and was probably charged with looking after the baby; Elizabeth Farrell from Co. Dublin was the nursery maid, responsible for the younger children; and Rose Matthews from Co. Louth was the house maid. Everyone in the household was a Roman Catholic and everyone (except for the youngest children) could read and write. They all spoke English and in addition the Lord Mayor and his mother-in-law spoke Irish. The Mansion House is described as a first-class dwelling with more than thirteen rooms.[81] The census in 1911 was taken on 2 April when the nationalist John Joseph Farrell was Lord Mayor. He was resident in the Mansion House with his wife Mary Josephine and their six children Eliza Mary (12), John (10), May Josephine (8), Eileen (6) Patrick (2) and the baby, Peter. There was one visitor on census night, a woman named Margaret Byrne. There were five servants: the House Steward Thomas Buckley and his wife Alice, both originally from Co. Galway; a nurse, Annie Maguire from Dublin City; and two domestic servants, Mary Anne Hughes and Maggie Clancy, both from Co. Wexford. Everyone was Roman Catholic and, with the exception of Alice Buckley and Annie Maguire, everyone spoke Irish as well as English.[82] The substantial complement of servants described in 1901 and 1911 must have been engaged and paid by the two Lord Mayors in question and were most likely domestic staff from their own residences. They were not employed by Dublin Corporation which although it did engage a housekeeper and cleaners for City Hall, did not provide any staff for the Mansion House.

Following the reunification of the Home Rule Party in 1900 under the leadership of John Redmond, most of the party's important meetings were held in the Mansion House Oak Room. As Lord Mayor, Timothy C. Harrington refused to present an address to King Edward VII when he visited Ireland in 1903, thus forfeiting a probable knighthood.[83] In the same year, Redmond convened secret meetings of senior party officials in the Mansion House Drawing Room to discuss the Wyndham Land Act and its likely effect on the country. These meetings were so confidential that they were held behind locked doors.[84] Lorcan Sherlock was Lord Mayor during the 1913 Lock Out and he 'opened a fund which gave food vouchers to the wives and dependants of the strikers' which was administered by the Lady Mayoress. [85] With the outbreak of World War I in 1914, Prime Minister

Timothy C. Harrington, Lord Mayor of Dublin 1901-03
Portrait by John Butler Yeats
Dublin Civic Portrait Collection

Mobile Recruiting Stand at the Mansion House 1915 with (in foreground) Band of the Irish Guards playing before deployment to the Front (From *Irish Life*)

H.H. Asquith came to Dublin to help with the recruitment drive and Redmond persuaded Lord Mayor Sherlock to allow a meeting to be held in the Mansion House Round Room. The Lord Mayor's secretary noted that 'the Redmondite Volunteers in uniform were acting as stewards at the meeting...there was a crowded audience in the Round Room. All present seemed to sympathise with the object of the meeting and there was a strong force of military outside.'[86] Sherlock's successor as Lord Mayor, Sir James Michael Gallagher, was more favourably disposed towards the war effort and he arranged for a mobile recruiting office to be placed on the Mansion House forecourt.

The Mansion House, and especially the Round Room, played its part in the movement towards independence which was triggered by the 1916 Rising. During this tumultuous period, the key figure was Lord Mayor Laurence O'Neill, who served from 1917 until 1924. During these troubled years he held the confidence of his fellow councillors: he was hailed in ballad as the greatest Lord Mayor since Daniel O'Connell and was viewed by some as the future president of an independent Irish Republic. O'Neill combined charm with oratorical gifts, political skill, mediation in industrial disputes, and a strong social conscience. In 1916 he was wrongfully imprisoned, an experience which gave him empathy with political prisoners and enabled him to be a successful negotiator between them and the authorities, especially in cases of hunger strike. On 19 April 1917 O'Neill convened an Irish Assembly in the Round Room to ensure that Ireland's position was submitted to the proposed Peace Conference following the end of the Great War. As Lord Mayor he convened and chaired the successful Mansion

House Conference against conscription, helping to unite all shades of nationalist opinion against this proposal. The first meeting of the Conference was held in the Mansion House on 18 April 1918 and was attended by most senior party representatives and Trade Union leaders. The strongly worded declaration, backed by the Catholic Church, encouraged Irish people to take a solemn pledge against the right of the British Government to enforce compulsory service in Ireland and to resist 'by the most effective means at our disposal'. More than one million people signed the pledge in parishes throughout Ireland.

A constitutional nationalist himself, O'Neill was friendly with both Eamon de Valera and Michael Collins and republican leaders secretly found shelter in the mayoral residence during the Troubles. On one occasion, Collins escaped detection when the British Army raided the Mansion House by posing as a janitor and sweeping the Round Room! [87] At the same time, Lord Mayor O'Neill cultivated the leading authorities on both the Irish and British sides so as to promote

National Pledge against Conscription Devised at Mansion House Dublin (Laurence O'Neill Papers)

openness to negotiation, employment and civic peace.[88] Following their landslide victory in the December 1918 General Election, Sinn Fein deputies refused to take their seat in Westminster and formed Dáil Eireann, which met for the first time in the Mansion House on Tuesday 21 January 1919 and declared Ireland's independence from Britain, and the Declaration of Independence was passed. For the rest of 1919, through 1920 and into 1921, the First Dáil continued to hold its meetings there while the Second Dáil held its first meeting in the Mansion House Oak Room on 16 August 1921. The Dáil Courts met occasionally in the Billiard Room (which is now used as staff offices) and the Minister for Local Government, W.T. Cosgrave, later used that room as his office, while De Valera used the Drawing Room as his.[89]

The War of Independence also began in January 1919. Hostilities between the Royal Irish Constabulary, bolstered by the Black & Tans and auxiliary forces, and the Irish Republican Army escalated dramatically at the end of 1920 and the death toll on both sides (including many civilians) mounted to over 1,000 victims. Both sides eventually agreed to enter peace talks in June 1921, and the terms of the Truce, marking the end of the Anglo-Irish War, were negotiated and signed in the Mansion House on 9 July 1921. The ensuing peace negotiations with the British Government ultimately led to the drafting of the Anglo-Irish Treaty, which allowed for the partition of Ireland. The Treaty was signed at a meeting of the Executive in the Mansion House Drawing Room on 6 December 1921. After animated debates, the Treaty was eventually approved by Dáil Eireann on 7 January 1922 by a narrow majority. It was ratified in the Mansion House on 14 January and a Provisional Government was elected.

In 1920, Dublin City Council moved to the Mansion House, where it was forced to remain for nearly four years while City Hall was under military

The First Dáil meets in the Mansion House Round Room
(National Library of Ireland)

The Second Dáil in session in the
Mansion House Round Room
(W.D. Hogan, Henry Street, Dublin)

occupation, first by the British army and later by the army of the Irish Free
State.[90] The Round Room was fitted out as a temporary council chamber,
furnished with benches from the real chamber in City Hall, which were
supplemented by sofas borrowed from the drawing room in the Mansion House.
The Lord Mayor's chair, another import from City Hall, lent a certain dignity to
the proceedings, which were overlooked by a motley gathering of civic
portraits assembled on the balcony of the Round Room and seeming to peer
down on deliberations.

Dublin City Council was suspended between May 1924 and October 1930 and
during this period the city did not have a Lord Mayor. As a result, the Mansion
House was only occupied by the House Steward for over six years and the
building required extensive refurbishment when the new Lord Mayor, Alfie
Byrne, was elected in 1930. As first citizen of Dublin, Byrne had a prominent part
to play in the Eucharistic Congress of 1932, when the papal legate, Lorenzo
Cardinal Lauri, stayed in the Mansion House and was conferred with the
honorary freedom of Dublin.

Because Byrne was Lord Mayor for nine consecutive terms of office, his
children grew up in the Mansion House and had fond memories of their happy
life there, which included sliding down the historic banisters and climbing onto
Van Nost's equestrian statue of George I, which was then in storage behind the
house – the Lord Mayor later ensured that the statue was transferred to the
Barber Institute in Birmingham, securing its future. Byrne's youngest child,
Sylvester Louis, was born while the family was resident in the Mansion House
and was presented with a cradle in solid silver by the employees of the famous
Irish Hospital Sweepstakes. Byrne was also famous for giving boxes of Urney
chocolates to children and young people and these were customised with a
picture of the Mansion House on the cover. He also kept postcards of the Mansion
House which he sent to admirers world-wide.

In 1938, a proposal was put forward which, if implemented, would have
seriously impinged on the Mansion House. This was put forward at a meeting

(Above) Priests attending the Eucharistic Congress photographed outside the Round Room entrance with Lorenzo Cardinal Lauri seated in front row (Dublin City Library & Archive, Greene Collection, image 175)

(Left) The only Native American priest to attend the Eucharistic Congress was Fr. Philip Gordon, shown here with Fr. J.J. Troy (*left*) and Lord Mayor Alfie Byrne outside the Mansion House (Dublin City Library & Archive, Greene Collection, image 59)

(Right) Box of Urney chocolates with customised cover given by Lord Mayor Alfie Byrne to young people

(Below) Postcard of the Mansion House sent by Lord Mayor Alfie Byrne to Terence Cox, Albany, New York, U.S.A. (Courtesy Seamas O Maitiu)

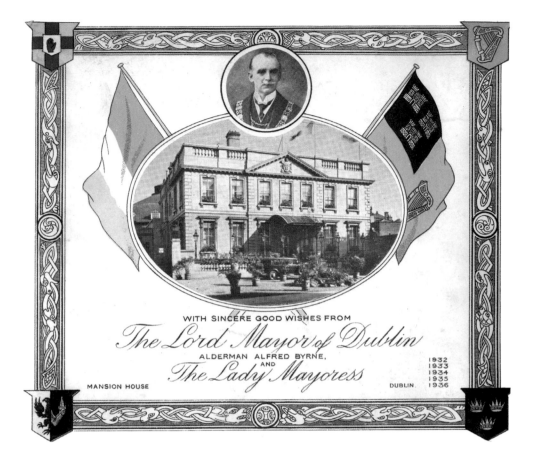

WITH SINCERE GOOD WISHES FROM

The Lord Mayor of Dublin

ALDERMAN ALFRED BYRNE, AND

The Lady Mayoress

MANSION HOUSE

1932
1933
1934
1935
1936

DUBLIN.

THE MANSION HOUSE. DUBLIN.

of Dublin City Council by the Labour Councillor, Martin O'Sullivan, seconded by Councillor Maud Walsh. He noted that the present accommodation for the Council's employees was inadequate and this combined with the ever-increasing scope of civic activities, meant that a new and larger City Hall was required. He further suggested that the City Manager, acting with the City Architect and newly-appointed Town Planning Consultants (Patrick Abercrombie, Sydney Kelly and Manning Robertson) should investigate the construction of a new City Hall, with particular reference to the site occupied by the present Mansion House. [91] However, when the consultants reported in 1941, the Mansion House was spared, as the consultants recommended that the new civic centre should include the existing City Hall, and should 'flank Parliament Street on the west, extending from Lord Edward Street to the Quays.'[92]

Alfie Byrne was succeeded in 1939 by the first woman Lord Mayor of Dublin, Caitlín Bean Uí Chléirigh, who was the widow of the 1916 leader and signatory of the Proclamation, Thomas J. Clarke, while her father Edward Daly had been a prominent member of the Fenian movement during the 19th century. She was one of the first women elected to such a post anywhere in the world, and there was huge international interest in her appointment. Understandably, Bean Uí Chléirigh's republican stance was uncompromising and her hatred of any connection with Britain was real and long-lasting. She steadfastly refused to wear the Lord Mayor's great chain, with its effigy of William III on the medal, and wore instead the simpler court of conscience chain, which bore no such royal likeness.[93]

Moving into the Mansion House on 19 July, Bean Uí Chléirigh's first action was to remove the portrait of Queen Victoria, which hung in the front hall, along with the three other royal portraits on display in the residence.[94] She even refused to allow these to be stored in the Mansion House, so the City Council had to make alternative arrangements to accommodate them.[95] This action provoked a storm of protest from many Dublin citizens, expressed through letters to national newspapers under pseudonyms such as *Patriotic Anti-Fanatic, A Southern Loyalist, Another Ratepayer* and *One Who Is Pained.*[96] The opposition of the Dublin ratepayers to this summary disposal of their property startled the Lord Mayor and may have governed her cautious response to a request asking her to donate the great chain and Victoria's portrait to the Ulster Protestant League in Belfast. She replied that since both those articles were the property of Dublin City Council, she had no control over their ultimate fate and advised the League to address its request to the Council. [97] Bean Uí Chléirigh was Lord Mayor when Dublin's North Strand was bombed by the Luftwaffe on 31 May 1941, a shocking incident made worse by the fact that Ireland was neutral in World War II. She immediately offered to house those made homeless in the Round Room until better accommodation could be provided for them.

The Mansion House was again at the centre of national life in 1948, when the First Inter-Party Government was formed following intensive negotiations in the Dining Room. The government was made up of a number of political parties including Fine Gael, the Labour Party, Clann na Poblachta, Clann na Talmhan and the National Labour Party. A plaque in the Dining Room commemorates this historic event. History was made again in 1956 when Robert Briscoe was elected as the first Jewish Lord Mayor of Dublin. A veteran of the

Caitlin Bean Ui Chleirigh
First woman Lord Mayor of Dublin 1939-41
(Photograph courtesy Helen Litton)

Irish War of Independence, Bob Briscoe carried out a hugely successful tour of the United States during his mayoralty, with large crowds gathered to see him wherever he went.

The tumultuous events of the period 1913–1924, and the suspension of Dublin City Council from 1924 to 1930, meant that the Lord Mayor's Ball fell into disuse. It was revived in October 1946 by Lord Mayor John McCann when it took place in the Metropole Ballroom, O'Connell Street, with the Lord Mayor's Coal Fund as the beneficiary. In October 1967, the Lord Mayor's Ball was revived yet again, when it was held in the R.D.S. Concert Hall in aid of St. Anne's Court Housing Scheme. In 1968 and 1969, the Lord Mayor's Ball was held on St. Patrick's Day at the Inter-Continental Hotel (later known as Jury's) in Ballsbridge, and the beneficiary was the Catholic Housing Aid Society. As there was no Lord Mayor in 1970-74 (Dublin City Council was suspended for failing to strike a rate) the

Lord Mayor Robert Briscoe (right) with Mayor
Richard J. Daley of Chicago, March 1957
(Dublin City Library & Archive,
Mayoral Photographs)

ball did not take place. However, it was revived yet again in 1975 and from then until 1997 the Lord Mayor's Ball took place on St. Patrick's Day in the Burlington Hotel, with the Central Remedial Clinic receiving the proceeds. The Lord Mayor's Ball, with proceeds going to charity, was revived by Naoise O Muírí in 2012 when it returned to the Mansion House and finally this new version of a very old tradition has continued since.

The Round Room and Supper Room were available for hire during the 20th century, and many and varied were the activities which took place there. Sales of work for almost every parish in Dublin; Irish dancing competitions, céilís on New Year's Eve and St. Patrick's Day, as well as Oireachtas competitions; art exhibitions and the Irish Antique Dealers' Fair; the Christmas Craft Fair and other Christmas celebrations, such as the inauguration of the Crib on 8 December.

The Round Room also saw its share of official events – the conferring of the Freedom of Dublin on the late Dr. Maureen Potter and Noel Purcell being a good example, or the Millennium Exhibition mounted by Dublin City Council during 1988. The Round Room and Supper Room now operate as a restaurant, which has become popular as a venue for wedding receptions.

Today, the Mansion House remains at the heart of Dublin's civic life. The ground floor is devoted to the official life of the residence. The Oak Room remains, as originally intended, as a venue for civic receptions and formal occasions. Each Lord Mayor adds his or her coat of arms to the walls of the Oak Room at the end of their term of office, beginning in 1841 with Daniel O'Connell and continuing to the present day. The Oak Room opens into the Drawing Room, where the Lord Mayor can relax informally with guests and then into the Blue Room, which is reserved for the Lady Mayoress. The formal rooms are completed by the Dining Room, and by the Lord Mayor's office. The main staircase, with its original barley-sugar balustrades in yew, leads to the first floor, where there

(Above) Irish Dancing Competition in the
Mansion House Supper Room
(Dublin City Library & Archive, Mansion
House Photographic Collection)

(Right) Two of Dublin's best-loved actors,
Noel Purcell and Maureen Potter receiving
the Honorary Freedom of the City
(Dublin City Library & Archive,
Honorary Freedom Photographs)

is an apartment for the Lord Mayor, and a separate apartment for the House Steward. A separate service stairs leads to the basement, which originally housed great kitchens and laundry rooms, but now is used mainly for storage as required. Most Lord Mayors live in the Mansion House and the warmth of family life adds a welcome informality to the residence. Ben Briscoe's daughter Rachel, a student of music at Trinity College, could often be heard playing the grand piano in the Drawing Room while her father was Lord Mayor while some years later Joe Doyle's tabby cat Smokey would descend the main staircase in a dignified manner to welcome guests.[98]

Several Lord Mayors have married during their term of office, and many have held their wedding receptions in the residence. The Mansion House is busier than it has ever been, with breakfast meetings often held there and receptions and events continuing throughout the day and well into the night. As it celebrates its three hundredth anniversary in 2015, Dublin's mayoral residence provides continuity and tradition, with a completely modern energy combined with old-fashioned warm hospitality: a fusion of the best elements of past and present which will serve the Mansion House well into the future.

Smokey waiting to welcome guests
to the Mansion House
(Courtesy Mrs. Peggy Doyle)

Former Lord Mayors with present Lord Mayor
Christy Burke Marking the 300th anniversary
of the Mansion House, January 2015

(Back row), *l-r* Gerry Breen, Michael Donnelly,
Catherine Byrne, Paddy Bourke, Oisin Quinn,
Eibhlin Byrne, Maurice Ahern, Dermot Lacey,
Naoise O Muiri, Andrew Montague,
Mary Freehill, Michael Mulcahy, Sean Haughey
and Brendan Lynch

(Front row l-r) Vincent Jackson, Michael
O'Halloran, Carmencita Hederman,
Lord Mayor Christy Burke, Fergus O'Brien,
Ben Briscoe and Emer Costello

THE MANSION HOUSE: HISTORICAL AND ARCHITECTURAL CONTEXT

Nicola Matthews

The Mansion House in its earliest manifestation was clearly conceived as a plain but prominent residence for self-promotion by an astute developer set on securing his place in society – but fate intervened abruptly disrupting Joshua Dawson's plans and undermining his achievement. The acquisition by Dublin city of the property from Dawson ensured that this early eighteenth century residence remained in continuous use as the centre of civic hospitality for the next three hundred years.

How this remarkable residence evolved into a complex of extraordinary civic buildings, now considered as a cultural site of national and international importance is best revealed through readily available historical mapping sources, the minutes of the Dublin City Assembly and the buildings themselves.

The first image of the house and its setting is to be found in Charles Brooking's map of Dublin city 1728, as one of several images of the prominent public buildings of the day. The Brooking map illustrates 'the Lord Mayor's House' as it was conceived as a prestigious Queen Anne style house, comprising two-storeys with a breakfront to the façade, consisting overall of seven bays with an unusual ornamented flat parapet set back from the street with curved flanking walls.

Following the lead of other early Dublin developers, Dawson gifted a site on Dawson Street to St. Ann's Parish to erect a church and vicarage.[2] The provision of a church signalled the establishment of an attractive and reputable neighbour-

(Left) The Lord Mayor's Garden is flanked by the Supper Room and the main residence. (Alastair Smeaton)

(Right)The earliest known elevation of Dublin's Mansion House From Charles Brooking's Map of Dublin 1728

hood. In this early part of the eighteenth century the Mansion House is framed to the north by St. Ann's Church – the two structures stand distinct and independent of the adjoining terraced streetscape of Dawson Street. This church is formally set to Dawson Street and appears to reference the baroque flanking walls of the formal forecourt or civic space to the front of the Lord Mayor's residence itself. The eighteenth century façade of the church is however instead only slightly set back from the street edge with shallow flanking curved walls on either side of the main facade. This baroque design was subsequently removed in the nineteenth century refurbishment of St. Ann's, which prompted the replacement of the early eighteenth century main façade in its entirety concealing the early origins of the parish church. As part of the overall master planning of his estate Dawson removed several buildings along the west side of Dawson Street to create linear connections to Grafton Street and the termination of Ann Street with the façade of St. Ann's church. Dawson's masterminding and control of this new street suggests that he was well versed in urban planning and desiring of a very distinctive character. The introduction of the 'courtly'

Plan of Lord Mayor's House and St. Ann's Church on Dawson Street with St. Stephen's Green in the background From Charles Brooking's Map of Dublin, 1728

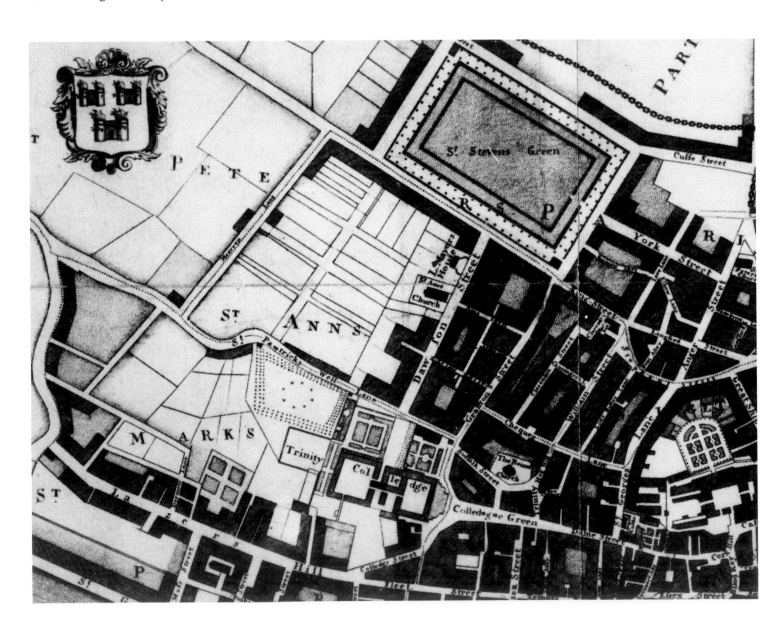

baroque style [3] indicates that Dawson was at least familiar with the work of eminent and influential English baroque architects of the day such as Sir Christopher Wren, who based their designs on research of the theories of classical antiquity. Dawson appears to have understood the concept that 'the organization of space is one manifestation of the organization of class and power'[4] and he clearly set about developing plans to attract aristocrats now returned to Dublin as part of the restored court of Charles II, and to encourage the settlement of this area in preference to other residential developments of the time, such as the prestigious Aungier estate. His success can be measured by the fact that the City Assembly first seriously considered purchasing Lord Longford's house in the Aungier estate as the Lord Mayor's residence, but decided instead to acquire Dawson's.

During the 1720s the Aungier estate was obliged to adjust to the migration of wealthier families from the larger buildings raised there in the 1660s to new houses on Dawson Street and St. Stephens' Green.[5] A measure of progress made is evident from the report in 1728 of objections from residents in Dawson Street regarding the 'great inconveniences' having erupted 'of late years by keeping up the ball at the Lord Mayor's house on St. Stephen's night', so much so that these celebrations were brought to an end.

With regard to the selected location of the property it is apparent from the following extract that the suitable conditions of the elevated site in close proximity to St Stephen's Green may well have encouraged development - Edward Southwell, writing to Joshua Dawson on 5 March 1712/3 is 'very glad to see your side of the water [south side of the Liffey] begin to take; and if you have so fundamental a reason as a dry foundation, you certainly must carry it if you could add the conveniency of a wooden bridge at Vanhumrys [Ferry] for coaches to go over; it would carry everything to your [side]'.[6]

Dawson's gamble to build a prominent and overtly ambitious residence as a political statement of his position and allegiance greatly exposed him when Queen Anne (his patron) died in 1714, leaving him with a suddenly inappropriate and unfashionable house. Dawson promptly set about realising his assets in order to turn his attentions to his country estate, Castledawson. Negotiations and the enhancement of his residence with an additional timber panelled reception room (the Oak Room) sealed the deal when he sold the house to the Dublin City Assembly in 1715.

Rocque's map of Dublin 1756 illustrates the residence, then known as 'Mayoralty House' at a prominent time in its history.

The scale of the Oak Room is clearly discernible, set slightly prominent of the building line to the rear of the main plan. The distinctive square plan of the original residence is evident, as are the front basement areas and the prominent forecourt.

The landscaping has evolved from wooded parkland to an enclosed space with a mannered lawn below a long raised terrace, situated along the north side of the house. The aspect over this formal garden was meant to be viewed and enjoyed from the principal reception rooms and not from the street as it is today. The Bowling Green to the rear of the property was a marker of social standing and denoted high-ranking gentlemen of the time. Development of adjoining land to the north and south of the Mansion House is evident.

The Mansion House
Detail from John Rocque's Map of Dublin, 1756

Clark's work on the Mansion House[7] notes that both interior and exterior of the house underwent major refurbishment works in the mid-eighteenth century. Dawson's original interiors were regarded as outdated and were revamped in line with new fashion. The commissioning of specific portraits for the Mansion House of Lord Lieutenants suggest the civic importance and role of the property as being integral in promoting the city's objective of Free trade and an independent parliament for Ireland.

Clark notes that the establishment of Grattan's Parliament in 1782 confirmed Dublin's status as the capital of Ireland and the second city of the Empire. The Dublin City Assembly, at pains to enhance the position of the Lord Mayor, provided a splendid new State coach, which was seen on the street for the first time in 1791. In tandem with the provision of the carriage, a coach house and stable yard was constructed on an adjoining garden to the south accessible from Dawson Street by a pair of arched carriage openings. A substantial stable yard is apparent and is central to a perimeter of coach houses and a street fronted Billets Office connected directly to the main residence, possibly in support of the role of the Lord Mayor's function in the collection of taxes.

Henry Shaw's Dublin Directory of 1850 depicts the impressive scale and architectural character of the Mansion House complex; the formal gardens and Bowling Green, the Billets Office, the stable and coach yard and the adjoining Baroque façade of St. Ann's Church – all integral parts of the earliest manifestation of the site.

Elevations on the east side of Dawson Street, including the Mansion House and St. Anne's (sic) Church
From Henry Shaw, Dublin Directory, 1850

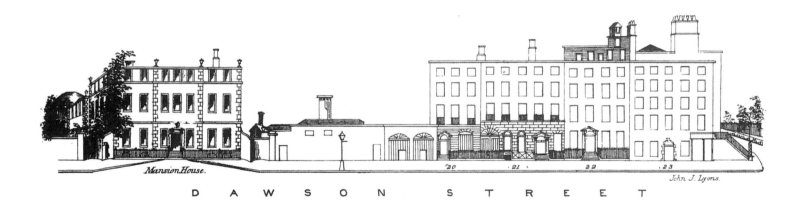

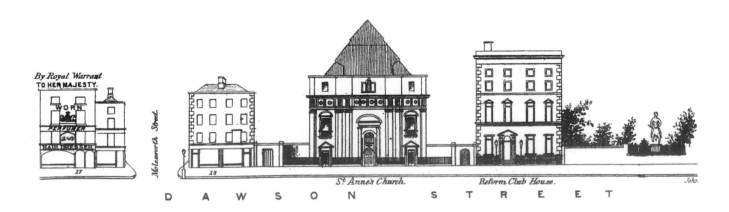

The importance and appropriateness of the architectural setting to the location of the equestrian statue of George I in the garden of the Mansion House is noted, the royal statue adding to the courtly character and status of the area when it was relocated to the Mansion House so that 'His Majesty' could relieve his boredom by 'looking over the wall' at people walking up and down Dawson Street[8]. The statue comprised a laurelled figure strongly classical in design and was lauded as 'a particularly fine piece'.

The Round Room beside the house was built in 1821 on part of the former Bowling Green to the rear of the house for a visit by King George IV. It was entered formally directly from the Oak Room initially. This internal processional route through the reception rooms of the residence changed subsequently over the years with the addition of new accommodation. The house originally occupied a considerable building plot with stables to the south and a large garden to the north side. The addition of the Supper Room in the latter part of the nineteenth century appears to be an attempt to keep up with the need to provide high standards of hospitality associated with the function of the Mansion House. Both of these structures have been operated separately in the past, but are linked by a corridor so that they can be interconnected as required for special events. State occasions appear to be the impetus for refurbishment and enhancement of the complex. The arrival of King George IV was no exception leading to the construction in 1821 of the King's Room (more commonly known as the Round Room) which was designed by John Semple, an eminent architect of the day, known for his extravagant church designs for the Board of First Fruits in Ireland.

The Round Room ' was intended to resemble the circular courtyard of an Arabian Palace. It is surrounded by a battlemented rampart about 22 feet high..... (and) the ceiling was painted to represent a sky.' This building would appear to be an overt reference to John Nash's Brighton Pavilion, the oriental and flamboyant Regency Palace commissioned by George IV in 1815 to host large social gatherings. The contractor selected to provide this structure was John Mountiford Hay which was due to his commitment to delivering the building on time. The speed of construction meant that the initial roof structure was of a temporary nature, and was only re-roofed properly a number of years later in 1824 also by John Semple. Ground plans by A. R. Neville of the room as built survive in the City Archives.

The room is ninety feet in diameter and fifty feet high and originally it was top lit by a lantern in the roof and dormer style windows at the upper level.[9] Its illusionistic interior was recorded by John Wilson Croker who described the room as arranged as 'the interior circular court of a Moorish palace open to the sky: the battlements were a gallery walled with ladies, music and a company of halberdiers, in Spanish dresses of light blue silk, as a guard of honour to the king.'

Towards the end of the 18th century the antiquated appearance of the Mansion House was drawing unfavourable comment such as this description in 1782: '... though [it is] a large good building [it] seems no way suitable for the mansion house of the chief magistrate of the great metropolis. It is a large old-fashioned house of brick, two storeys high containing a range of seven windows in each storey but is of considerable depth from the street backwards.' Thackeray's description in 1843 was particularly damning, 'a queer old dirty brick house.....' In the early 19th century, the aspirations of the city to raise the profile and stature

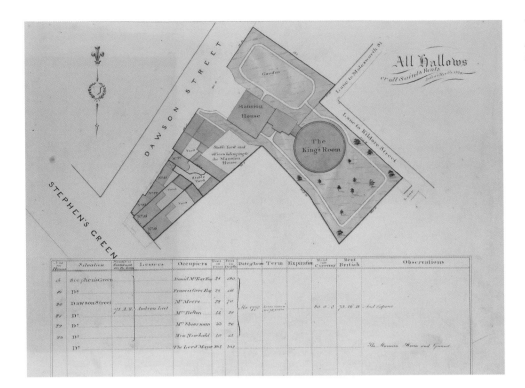

A.R. Neville's Atlas of Dublin City Estates, 1829, showing the Mansion House and its grounds (Dublin City Library and Archive)

of the Lord Mayor during a period of economic downturn by improving the mayoral residence were dependent upon offering speculative opportunities for development. Historical survey maps dated 1812 describe proposals for demolition of the Mansion House and full re-development of its site for terraced townhouses aligned to new streets. Serious consideration was given to relocating the Lord Mayor's residence to a site at the centre of Stephen's Green thus addressing the deficits of the Green's interior while improving its function as a civic space. However these options did not gain favour and Dawson's Mansion House remained the residence of the Lord Mayor.

The Round Room underwent extensive renovation in 1892 carried out to the designs of Spencer Harty in consultation with the architect Charles Ashlin. The contractor was Sibthorpe & Son. A description in *The Builder* (June, 1892) of the interior records that the ceiling had been remodelled and a new cornice added with sixteen circular windows underneath, which were leaded lights of tinted cathedral glass. On either side of the windows were thirty-two shields represented each county of Ireland. Architectural details are picked out in white and gold. The architrave is supported by pilaster in enamelled wood coloured red and gold. The walls and railings of the balcony were stained in old gold with ornamental gilding. The first Dail Eireann assembled here in 1919 – a scene vividly evoked in Tom Ryan's painting that hangs above the entrance to the present Dail chamber. The Victorian pilasters, gallery and dais were replaced c.1940 by a concrete gallery and stage.

The Supper Room was constructed in the late nineteenth century as a venue to provide additional hospitality for the functions of the Mansion House and the Round Room. The original building was exuberant in style, an impressive single volume space set on the same level as the ground floor of the main house and elevated to look out over and to integrate the residence with the garden by

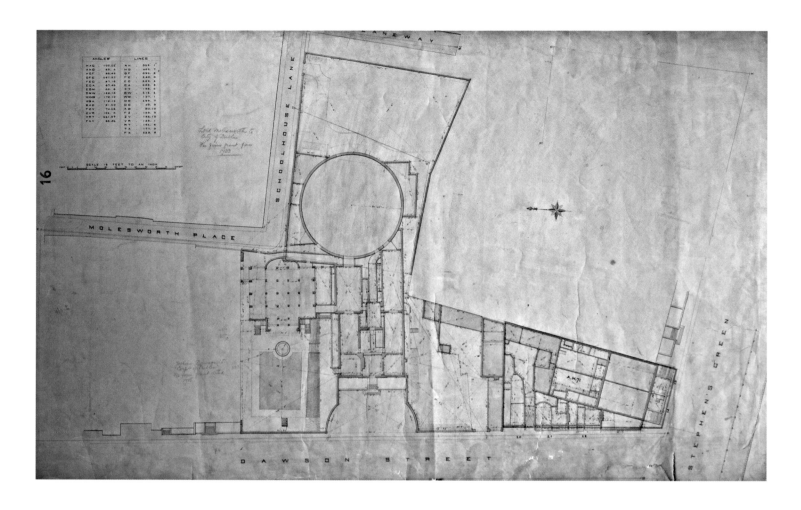

Dublin City Estate Map, 1908, showing plan of Mansion House Residence, Round Room and Supper Room (Survey & Mapping Office, Dublin City Council)

way of a cascading staircase. The building was of considerable architectural quality (referenced to Osborne House, Isle of Wight) and provided a dining room with an impressive well-lit spatial quality that is still enjoyed today in its current use as a restaurant. The room has a timber-trussed roof supported on ornate cast iron columns with a stained glass clerestory over the 'nave' section, side aisles with lean-to roofs and a curved 'apse-like' end wall. The original building presented an architecturally interesting gable with a recessed façade arranged to a raised viewing terrace and staircases that connected directly to the garden. The Supper Room was interconnected to the other reception rooms of the Mansion House along the north elevation of the Oak Room by way of an open court retaining the basement area and natural light to the original windows of this elevation of the Oak Room.

The terrace and stairs were removed in a later addition to the garden front in the 1930s. Alterations were also made at this time that included a new entrance to the Round Room with an enclosed connection being made between the Oak Room and the Supper Room. Changes to the forecourt at a similar date resulted in the loss of the earlier enclosing walls and the widening of the forecourt to the north to create a new entrance to the Round Room as well as opening up the private garden to the street with a railed boundary. A multi-story car park was built to the rear on Schoolhouse Lane in the 1990s and a commercial office block, Joshua Dawson House, was more recently developed on the south side on the site of the former stables and yard.

The Lord Mayor's Garden

The Lord Mayor's Garden is located on the north side of the house. The garden was originally surrounded by a high wall and was not visible from the street being a formal pleasure ground for the enjoyment of the Lord Mayor, his family and guests. The windows on the north side of the house, from the drawing room and parlour, overlook the garden. On John Rocque's 1756 map the layout of the garden shown is an elegantly simple one with a lawn, an embanked flight of steps and wide paths. The lawn is the dominant feature and is divided in two by the central path leading from the house. The curve of the perimeter wall to the forecourt of the house is echoed in the shape of the border and the lawns at their south ends. The bowling green is shown to the rear of the house adjacent to the garden. By the early Victorian period, as shown on the 1847 Ordnance Survey map, the garden has become more symmetrical in design. The Round Room has been built on the site of the Bowling Green and the lawn depicted on Rocque's map has been replaced by two rectangular cultivated plots shown as 'parterre' style beds. The plot on the west side is divided into quadrants, all bounded by 'boxed' hedging. The other longer rectangular plot is divided by diagonal paths, creating a 'St. Andrew's Cross' pattern of four triangular shaped beds. The beds are edged with hedging. Perimeter borders are marked on the west, north and east sides of the garden though no trees or shrubbery are depicted. Van Nost's equestrian statue (1722) of King George I having been relocated from Essex Bridge is indicated at the edge of the west border.[10] By 1864 the Supper Room has been added and the three perimeter borders have been widened. The west border now incorporates the statue of George 1. A row of well-spaced deciduous trees is shown along the north boundary. The east and

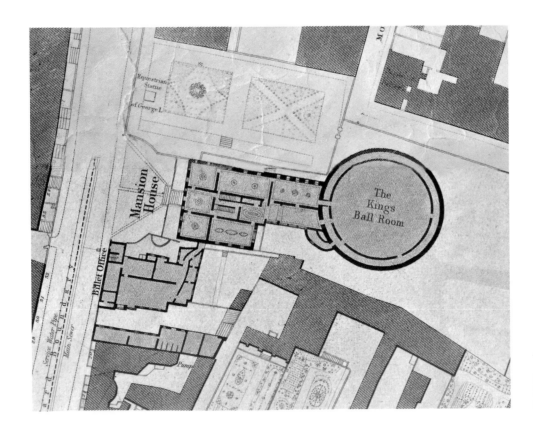

Detail of Ordnance Survey Map of Dublin 1847 showing the Mansion House, Round Room and Lord Mayor's Garden

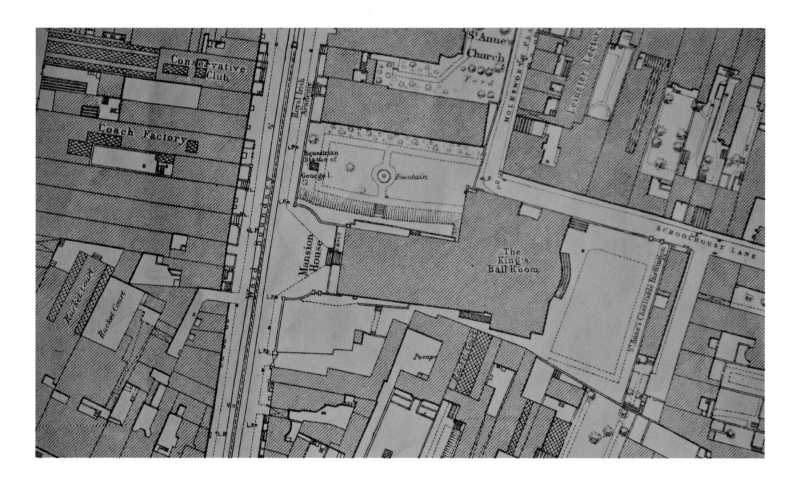

(Above) Detail of Ordnance Survey Map of Dublin 1872 showing the Mansion House, Round Room and Lord Mayor's Garden

(Overleaf) The Lord Mayor's Garden with central fountain (Joanna Travers)

west sides of the garden are also planted with trees in a linear sequence, four to the east and four to the west. The garden is still walled and no entrance is evident in the curved section of wall at the forecourt.

The 1872 map shows changes to the layout and the two central beds have been replaced with lawns once more. The flight of steps has increased from five to six steps and is now aligned with the central path, which has been widened and at its halfway point forms a circular curve to accommodate a new fountain and basin.

The row of trees on the north border has been replaced by mixed shrubbery. The west border still has three trees depicted, two now at the south end and one at the north end. Twentieth century maps do not record the garden layout or contents except for the fountain and the statue. The statue of George I has been removed according to the 1936 Ordnance Survey edition map and a new garden front has been added to the Supper Room. In the twenty first century, the Lord Mayor's Garden has been transformed as part of the recent works to the former Supper Room. The new layout of the garden has been developed as a collaborative design process between Dublin City Council and Sean Harrington Architects with Shaffrey Associates and Finola Reid as historic garden consultants.

THE MANSION HOUSE: AN ARCHITECTURAL SURVEY

Susan Roundtree

Architectural style, patron and influences

The Mansion House, purchased for use as a Mayoralty House by Dublin Corporation from Joshua Dawson in 1715, is the earliest continuously occupied town house in Dublin. It is one of the most important historic buildings in the city because of its age and unique architectural style, and for the continuous role the house has played in the civic history of Dublin. It is also the oldest surviving mayoral residence in either Britain or Ireland. In this chapter we look at the architecture of the house and the particular features that illustrate its very special character.

As outlined in the introductory chapters, the house was built by Joshua Dawson on land he acquired for the development of the area in 1705. It was completed in about 1710 to a design influenced by the Queen Anne or English Baroque style of architecture.[1] The house has a sophisticated square plan with the main rooms arranged *en filade* around two centrally located staircases. The roof design, which is original, is most unusual. It comprises a series of low slated pitches running from front to rear concealed behind what was originally a solid panelled parapet. The position of the house set back from the street with curved flanking walls is a significant and unusual feature for a Dublin town house of the early eighteenth century. The house was originally faced with brick with stone quoins emphasising the corners and sweeping steps to a carved stone entrance door case. The windows on both ground and first floor are of similar size and proportion. Their box frames would originally have been flush with the outside brickwork, as indicated in the Brooking view of 1728.[2]

The unusual style of the house with its baroque features has been explained by the social and political allegiances of its owner and patron, Joshua Dawson, who was a known Tory and loyal support of Queen Anne. It is suggested that he may have designed the house himself, making a particular statement about his influence, position and wealth. With the untimely death of Queen Anne in 1714, Joshua Dawson left his position in Dublin Castle. He offered his Dublin house for sale to the City Assembly at a cost of £3,500 sterling. Under the purchase agreement, Dawson was required to build an additional large assembly room for the Corporation and to wainscot, paint and finish it completely. This room subsequently became known as the Oak Room and is still used

A dramatic view of a Waterford crystal chandelier in the Oak Room (Conor McCabe)

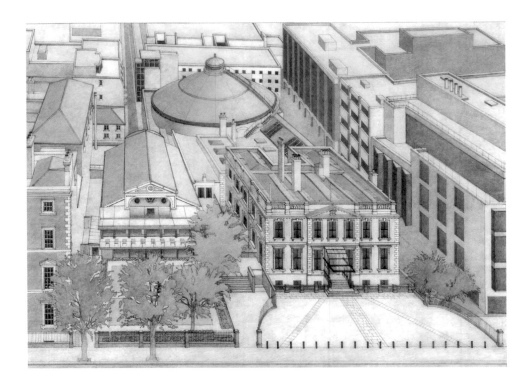

(Left) Perspective drawing of Mansion House, Round Room and Supper Room in 2015 Drawing by Mark Costello

(Below) Plan of Mansion House with original edifice highlighted. Drawing by Mark Costello

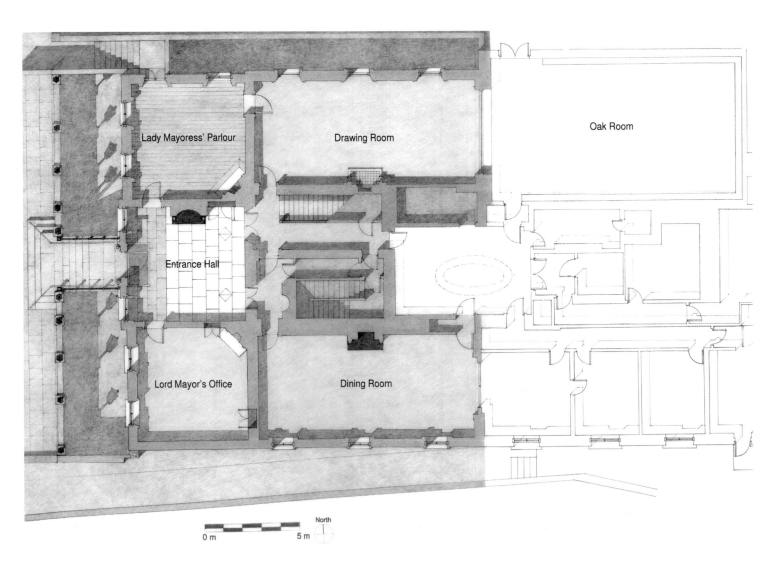

Lady Mayoress' Parlour

Drawing Room

Oak Room

Entrance Hall

Lord Mayor's Office

Dining Room

North

0 m   5 m

Cross section through the Mansion House
Drawing by Mark Costello

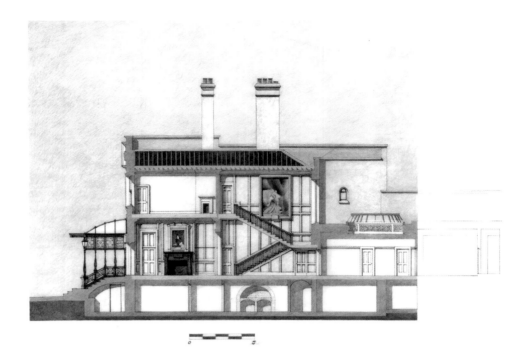

today for civic receptions. Dawson agreed to leave the house and outhouses in good repair with brass locks and marble chimney pieces retained and he gave assurance of a secure, undoubted and uncontested title. He was required to leave existing furnishings in many of the rooms. These are described in the conveyance agreement and include tapestry hangings, silk, scarlet calamanco and Indian calico window curtains, window seats, chimney glasses and gilt leather hangings in the walnut parlour. The conveyance was signed and sealed on 18 May 1715.[3]

The Mansion House is of modest size with two stories of accommodation over a sunken basement floor. It is seven bays wide with a deep, almost square, floor plan. The roof consists of a series of low pitched sections running front to rear and not visible from the street. Charles Brooking's view of the house from 1728 shows the original form of the front façade with its panelled parapet crowned with decorative urns and decorated with statuary. The house sat on its own grounds with gardens to the north and south. The plot was increased in 1733 when land behind the house was acquired from Viscount Molesworth. Three years later this land was seeded for use as a bowling green. John Rocque's map of 1756 shows the house with the Oak Room, a substantial garden to the side and the bowling-green to the rear. Stables on the north side were constructed in 1778 and these are shown on the manuscript Wide Streets Commissioners map of 1781. A coach house for the new Lord Mayor's coach was constructed in 1791.[4]

The house is constructed with a stone basement and with brick walls above this level. It was originally faced with brick. The carved stone entrance door case shown in the Brooking view was changed to one of classical design in about 1783. Simon Vierpyl is credited with carving the Portland stone door case that survives today which has two engaged Ionic columns supporting an entablature with a pulvinated frieze and modillion cornice below a triangular pediment.[5]

(Left) Lord Mayor's House from Charles
Brooking's Map of Dublin 1728
Coloured in red by Susan Roundtree to
show its original appearance in brick

(Below) Wide Streets Commission Map showing
Mansion House Ground, 1781
Image coloured by Susan Roundtree

(Right)Georgian porch attributed to
Simon Vierpyl enclosed by Victorian portico
designed by Daniel Freeman
(Alastair Smeaton)

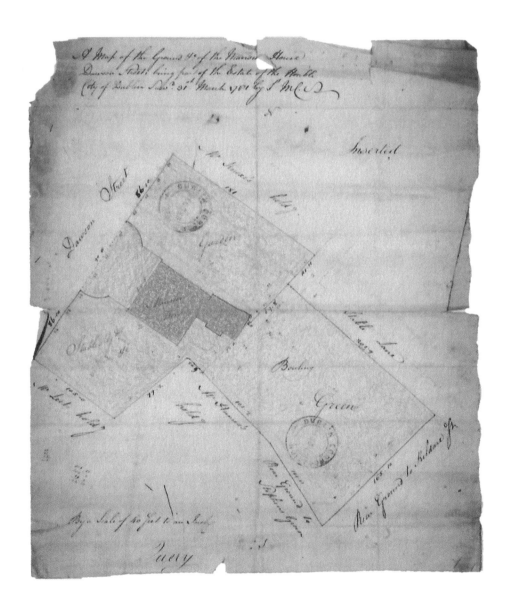

Portico designed by City Architect Daniel Freeman
Photograph from The Irish Builder, 1896

An anonymous description of the house, from 1782, notes that 'it is a large… house of brick, two stories high containing a range of seven windows in each storey but is of considerable depth from the street backwards. The roof is concealed by a parapet wall, adorned with urns, and the apartments are large and elegant'.[6] Most early eighteenth century town houses had visible and steeply-pitched roofs, so the unusual appearance of the house attracted comment, much of it critical.[7] Campbell, writing in 1775, refers to the unusual window proportions of the house.[8] Wright, in 1825, describes it as 'unprepossessing, being fronted entirely in brick, and built after a design which never could have been pleasing to the eye'.[9] Thackeray, visiting Dublin in 1843, writes that he had 'just passed his lordship's mansion in Dawson Street – a queer old dirty brick house with dumpy urns at each extremity and looking as if a storey of it had been cut off – a rasée-house'.[10] Ball describes the house as a 'low edifice, unworthy of its appropriation, and ill according with the other public buildings in the metropolis.' He continues 'It is situated in a recess in Dawson-street, presenting a mean brick front, and distinguished principally by being the most unsightly edifice in the street in which it stands.'[11]

Critical and unflattering comments like these may have been the impetus to transform the front façade of the house to a Victorian style in the mid nineteenth century. This façade dominates its appearance today and visitors are often surprised that the house has such early origins. The façade renewal, undertaken in 1851, was carried out to a design by the city architect, Hugh Byrne. It radically altered the façades of the house by concealing the eighteenth century brick with render and adding decorative surrounds to the ground and first floor windows on the front façade and part of the north side facing the garden.[12] The window sashes were altered and the solid parapet on the front façade was replaced with a stone balustrade with cast iron balusters and a pediment decorated with the Lord Mayor's coat of arms.[13] The railings to the front area were also replaced with the present stone balustrade and cast iron balusters, topped with cast-iron lamps and lanterns similarly decorated with the arms of the Lord Mayor. The decorative cast and wrought iron porch, which originally had a coloured glass roof, was added in 1886. It was designed by the city architect, Daniel Freeman, and manufactured by leading metal work fabricators, Messrs J & C McGloughlin.[14]

Paint samples taken from the front façade recently show that the paint layers and substrate at the parapet level differ from lower parts of the façade.[15] This indicates that the parapet section was rendered first, possibly because of its poor condition and this, in turn, may have been a further influencing factor in deciding to render the rest of the façade and transform the appearance of the house. The Victorian façade treatment is, however, relatively superficial and features of the earlier house are still apparent when it is viewed from the north and south sides where flush sash boxes and sections of panelled parapet survive. On the south side in particular, narrow first floor window openings are original although now fitted with nineteenth century sashes.

Construction detail and special features

While the external appearance of the house has radically changed since 1715, internally much survives to confirm its early origin. These are most notably elements of early eighteenth century construction, detail and structural arrangement. Massive timber beams span from front to back with floor joists and independent ceiling joists spanning between the main beams with morticed connections.

A flat plaster and lath ceiling was adhered to these lower ceiling joists with a timber cornice that survives in a number of areas. This is consistent with the typical framed construction described by Arthur Gibney and noted in other early eighteenth century Dublin buildings such as Marsh's Library, Trinity Library and Dr Steevens' hospital. By the 1740s Irish carpenters had abandoned the use of framed floors entirely and moved to long span joists instead as these were found to be more economical.[16]

Internal and external masonry walls above basement level are constructed in brick. Brickwork is visible behind the shutters in the drawing room and has also been noted behind the paneling in the hall and in the attic roof space. This is consistent with the use of brick as the material of choice for domestic

Detail of original beam, first floor
(Dublin City Council Architect's Section)

Original beams in attic showing carpenters' marks
(Susan Roundtree)

buildings of the early eighteenth century in Dublin. The bricks are likely to have been made locally as bricks were being manufactured in the city at the time in several locations. Brickfields in Ringsend, for example, are recorded in the Pembroke Estate Papers in 1706.[17]

At roof level the original beam construction from front to back survives and is consistent with the structure of the rest of the house. The roof has five adjacent pitched roofs with ridges running front to back. This gives a low ridge line which is not visible from ground level. The parapets are sloped on the inside and slated and there is an early reference to this particular detail in the city records.[18] The presence of rough timbers, carpenter marks and no ridge board used in the forming of the roof confirm its early date. The original beams appear to be of red deal (Pinus Sylvestris). This species, also known as Baltic pine or Redwood, was commonly imported from Scandinavia and the Baltic countries. It was not native to Ireland at that time and this would appear to be a relatively early use of it for building construction as previously oak, usually sourced in Ireland, was the dominant structural species.[19] Some of the constructional details also confirm an early date – the use of heavy sections and both mortice and tenon and halving lap joints with trenails or pegs. There is also evidence of alteration and repair at various times – the use of welded steel strapping, plating and bolting through of decayed beam ends, and more recently the use of North American Spruce for repairs. At the rear of the roof there are hip ends with cast iron roof lights which appear to be a later addition.

Originally there were four chimneystacks but one of the front pair has been removed. The fireplaces generally in the house appear to have caused on-going problems and most of them associated with the early house have been altered, the exception being the entrance hall fireplace.

Eighteenth-century polished limestone
fireplace in Entrance Hall
(Susan Roundtree)

The main stairs, from ground to first floor, is a particularly fine example of a dog-leg open string staircase, an unusual design for this date,[20] but confirmed to be original to the 1710 house by its construction and detail with a wide moulded handrail and large square newel posts. The balusters are hand carved tapered barley twist columns with three columns dovetailed into each tread board. Most unusually the handrail and balusters are made from yew wood (Taxus Baccata), a very rare timber to be used for joinery work.[21] The handrail has a moulded top section applied in a cross-grained direction. The tread end brackets are hand carved with a floral design. The handrail is unpainted but the balustrade has at least eight layers of paint that conceal the appearance of the timber beneath.

The secondary staircase, which serves all floors, is also original to 1710 and has an unusual baluster design of a style not encountered elsewhere. Scrutiny of the existing fabric suggests that the secondary staircase, which now terminates at the first floor, may originally have extended to roof level to a viewing platform, a further feature of the Queen Anne style.

At first floor level, while the plan arrangement of rooms can still be discerned, very few eighteenth century interior features survive. In one or two concealed places original paneling and a timber cornice survive and there are some early windows on the south side with raised and fielded shutters and window seats. The need to cater for residential uses at first floor has led to greater change at this level with the insertion of bathroom and kitchen facilities.

At basement level the footprint of the original 1710 house with the Oak Room addition is clearly discernible. Historical accounts suggest that the fabric at basement level suffered early on from damp, which prompted the early excavation of basement areas to alleviate the pressure on the basement walls. In 1765 the terrace around the house was removed and replaced with an area to resolve dampness.[22]

(Left) Main staircase original to the
Mansion House
(Alastair Smeaton)

(Above) Main Staircase in Mansion House
viewed from top landing with 'barley-sugar'
balusters and original panelling in
Staircase Hall
(Susan Roundtree)

(Right) Secondary staircase original
to the Mansion House
(Alastair Smeaton)

Description of interior (and later changes)

Internally the style of the house reflects the many changes that have taken place to the building over its 300 year history. The changes include repair work and refurbishment, alterations and additions, and stylistic changes to suit the differing tastes of the house's occupants and custodians. The interior represents a layering of history that is important in its own right and, in many instances, is associated with significant events that have taken place in the house.

In the purchase agreement, Dawson agreed to leave the house and outhouses in good repair with twenty four brass locks and six marble chimney pieces retained. In the early eighteenth century brass locks were customarily moved (with fire grates) from house to house and not considered to be fixtures. For this reason they are often mentioned in early inventories and would be a normal item to be found in a 'quality' house, as would marble chimney pieces. Dawson also agreed to leave existing furnishings in some rooms. These included tapestry hangings, silk window curtains and window seats and a chimney glass in the great bed-chamber, items that indicate that this was an expensively-furnished room. Fabrics were much valued at the time, as were chimney glasses or mirrors, which were also present in the walnut parlour, Dantzick oak parlour and the large eating room. It is obvious that Dawson took great care with the choice of furnishings for his house. Gilt-leather hangings were expensive and fashionable in the early eighteenth century. Lord Powerscourt had them in the hall of his Dublin house in the 1720s. A sense of style is also indicated in matching window seat coverings with curtains as noted in the description of the Danzick oak parlour which was used as a drawing room. Research has found that red (all shades) was the most popular colour for drawing rooms in the eighteenth century although the fabrics, calamanco[23] and Indian calico, were not particularly expensive.[24]

Surviving features also indicate that the house was well finished internally with all main rooms panelled and wainscoted as would be expected in a house of this date.[25] The timber panelling was fixed to timber frames directly onto brickwork. Oak was the most usual timber for panelling, either imported or home grown.[26] In the 1715 description of the house rooms are named according to their panelling, for example the Danzick oak parlour and the walnut parlour. Today timber panelling survives only in the entrance hall and main staircase hall although associated elements of panelling – timber cornice and oak window surrounds and seats – survive in the Lord Mayor's study, whose walls remained panelled until the 1970s. Fragments of timber cornice also survive at first floor in the staircase hall and concealed above a later ceiling. The Oak Room, originally panelled in Danzick oak, still has an oak panelled interior although the room has been greatly altered and was substantially remodelled in 1934.[27]

Recently carried out paint analysis of the interior has provided information on how decorative schemes in the house changed over time.[28] The earliest schemes involved dark brown paint on the back stairs, pale stone colours or off-white in the main staircase hall and entrance hall, off-white in the drawing room, and pinks in the first floor parlour. The original decoration was largely repeated through the rest of the eighteenth and first half of the nineteenth century. As the nineteenth century progressed, more colours were used. These were mostly pale greens but there were some pinks and blues and one violet scheme in the first floor parlour. The main changes took place in the main staircase hall and entrance hall which started the nineteenth century in stone colours and off-whites but ended up dark brown by the end of the century. In the second half of the twentieth century most rooms were painted in pale tones except for the main staircase hall which was consistently painted dark brown. In recent years colour schemes for the main public rooms have been devised with the benefit of technical paint analysis and considerable historical research.

Internal additions and improvements to make the drawing room 'more commodious and ornamental' were suggested in 1763.[29] The success of these works prompted similar alterations to the south side rooms carried out in 1765. This date is consistent with the style of joinery that survives today in the dining room. The work carried out included the insertion of a bow window in the end wall of the dining room and the creation of a basement area on each side of the house to alleviate dampness in the basement rooms.[30]

Initially the Round Room, constructed in 1821, connected directly with the Oak Room. A second passage between the house and the Round Room was added in 1830. A new single-storey Supper Room, designed by the architect Hugh Byrne, was added in 1864 and completed before Christmas that year.[31]. This first Supper Room, as described in the *Dublin Builder*, was sixty feet long by twenty two feet wide and connected to the Dining Room by 'handsome folding doors'. The room was later used for billiards when the Supper Room was relocated to its present position in the 1890s. In the early twentieth century the space was converted to a guest bedroom wing. Today these rooms are administrative offices for the Lord Mayor's staff in the house.

In 1900, probably in anticipation of Queen Victoria's visit to Dublin in April that year, a significant scheme of redecoration and renovation was carried out to the Mansion House and the Round Room under the direction of the city architect, Charles J. McCarthy.[32] The panelled ceiling in the entrance hall was installed, the drawing room was refurbished and the spectacular stained glass window from the Joshua Clarke studio was commissioned for the main staircase hall. The drawing room refurbishment included the additional of ornamental plasterwork and the installation of electric light chandeliers, called 'electroliers'. The works were carried out by the important interior design contractors, Henry Sibthorpe & Son.[33] Interior photographs of the key public rooms in the house exist from this period, a valuable record of the decorative schemes of the main reception rooms in the early twentieth century. Many features of this period, such as plasterwork, chandeliers, lamps and fire screens, are still in the house. A very detailed colour wash drawing of the house and grounds also survives from this period.[34]

A further important phase of renovation in the house took place in the 1930s. The Mansion House had been vacant for a number of years and had fallen into poor condition. Renovation works were planned and carried out following the election of Alfie Byrne as Lord Mayor in 1930. The works included significant structural repairs, such as the addition of steel beams to support the floors over the Dining Room, and the creation of additional bedrooms in the former billiards room for visitors during the Eucharistic Congress 1932.[35]

Extensive remodelling of the Oak Room was also carried out, made necessary as a result of changes to improve access to the Round Room and Supper Room. A new entrance lobby to these public rooms had a significant impact on the Oak Room. In the remodelling of the room at this time the windows on the north side were blocked up and the room was re-roofed with roof lanterns and lay lights to provide natural light. A good deal of the current panelling in the room dates from this particular period of change.[36] The forecourt was also changed. It was widened to the north to provide a separate gated entrance to Round Room and Supper Room.

The Round Room & Supper Room

Many changes to the Mansion House have resulted from the addition of the public rooms that are known as the Round Room and Supper Room. The Round Room, as it is known today, was constructed for the visit of King George IV in 1821 and, as described in earlier chapters, its speed of its construction was remarkable. The architect was John Semple and the contractor was John Mountiford Hay.[37] The room is ninety feet in diameter and fifty feet high and was originally top lit by a lantern in the roof and dormer windows at the upper level.[38] It was roofed temporarily for the king's visit and work to complete the Round Room continued for some years to make it a more permanent structure. This involved roofing works, glazing works and ventilation works. Dr Anthony Meyler, a leading expert on sanitation and ventilation, was consulted in 1822.[39] In 1824 both the Round Room and the Mansion House had gas lighting installed and in 1830 a second passage was constructed to connect the two buildings.

The architect, Hugh Byrne, was the designer of works carried out in 1855. These are described in *The Irish Builder*, which notes that the 'interior has been painted, and the canvas roof decorated with panels and a cornice at (the) foot. Pilasters rise from the gallery to the roof and on the former an ornamental iron railing is fixed'.[40]

Mansion House Round Room as it appeared between 1900 and 1939 (National Library of Ireland, Eason Collection)

The Round Room underwent further renovation in 1892 carried out to the plans of Spencer Harty, Borough Engineer, assisted by the architect George Coppinger Ashlin. The contractors were Sibthorpe & Son. A description in *The Irish Builder* notes that 'the ceiling has been remodeled and a new cornice added with sixteen circular windows underneath which are leaded lights of tinted cathedral glass.'[41]

The additional windows addressed what was perceived to be the poor lighting of the building in the original design. On either side of the windows were added thirty two shields representing each county of Ireland. Architectural details were picked out in white and gold. The architrave was supported by new pilasters in enamelled wood, which were coloured red and gold. The walls and railings of the balcony were stained in old gold with ornamental gilding.'[42]

Initially the Round Room was connected directly to the Oak Room. This connection remained in place until about 1900. At that time the main doorway to the Round Room was given a new ornamental over-door with the city arms as part of general redecoration and renovation works carried out under the direction of the city architect, Charles McCarthy.[43] The elaborate over-door can be seen in the photograph of the First Dáil meeting in the room, which took place on 21st January 1919. The Round Room was remodeled again in the 1930s when the Victorian pilasters, gallery and dais were replaced by a concrete gallery and stage and the covered passageway connecting the Oak Room, Round Room and Supper Room was constructed.

As previously noted, the first Supper Room was constructed as an extension to the house in 1864 to the design of the city architect, Hugh Byrne, located to the rear of the Dining Room on the south side of the house. In 1881 the need for a larger Supper Room was identified and addressed by building temporary accommodation in the garden on the north side of the house. However, by 1884 this temporary room was considered to be both a hazard and a disfigurement and a letter received from the President of the Royal Irish Academy in that year expressed concern about possible danger to the institution and its contents from the proximity of this inflammable timber supper room structure. It was agreed that this building should not be allowed to disfigure the Mansion House any longer and should be demolished.[44]

In 1891 plans were approved for the erection of a permanent Supper Room on the garden site where the temporary building had stood.[45] The architect George Ashlin was engaged to design the new building because the City Architect was incapacitated by illness.[46] The new Supper Room was constructed by the Corporation's own building staff at a cost of £2,400 and was completed in early 1892.[47] George Coppinger Ashlin was an important architect in Dublin in the latter years of the nineteenth century. He was arguably the leading church architect in the country at this time and played an active role in the affairs of the architectural profession in Ireland, becoming president of the RIAI in 1902. In his early career Ashlin was articled to Edward Pugin and ran the Irish office of Pugin & Ashlin, which specialised in churches, convents and monasteries.[48] The Supper Room survives and is the core of the popular restaurant that now occupies the site. The interior has some church-like features but is an impressive single volume space in an exuberant architectural style. The Supper Room is level with the ground floor of both the Mansion House and the Round Room and elevated to look out over the garden. It is well-lit with a timber trussed roof supported on ornate cast iron columns and a stained glass clerestory over the 'nave' section. It has side aisles with lean-to roofs and a curved 'apse-like' end wall. The building as designed presented a strong gable to Dawson Street with a west-facing viewing terrace and a pair of symmetrical staircases that connected directly from the terrace to the garden. The original façade can be seen in early twentieth century photographs, such as the First Dáil Executive Council photograph (1919) and the Lawrence Collection Frozen Fountain image of c.1900.

The original layout of the Supper Room, and its connections with the Round Room and Mansion House, is shown on the City Estate map of c.1900. The terrace and stairs were removed when the west façade of the building was

Two views of the frozen fountain in Mansion House Garden, c. 1900 (National Library of Ireland, Laurence Collection)

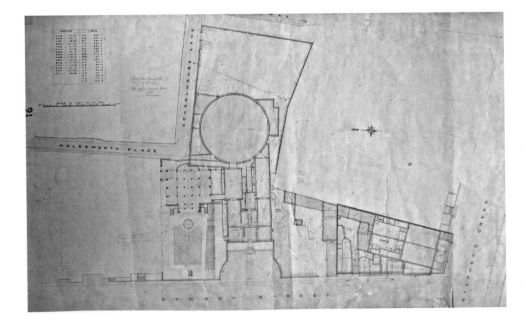

Plan of the Mansion House, shown on City Estate Map, 1900 (Photo: Alastair Smeaton)

The Lord Mayor's Garden,
showing new façade of Supper Room
(Alastair Smeaton)

extended and given a new front and larger terrace in the 1930s which included the creation of a separate entrance to the Round Room from the forecourt. The enclosing walls of the garden were also replaced with railings at this time opening up the garden to the street as a public space.

The Lord Mayor's Garden, located on the north side of the house, was originally surrounded by a high wall and not visible from the street. In this way it served as a formal pleasure ground for the enjoyment of the Lord Mayor, his family and guests. Today the garden is a much more public space and has been transformed by recent works to the Supper Room which have reinstated the layout of the original forecourt to the main house. The Round Room and Oak Room are now served by a new separate access route from the street on the south side of the garden. On the northern boundary a new pedestrian access has been provided to the serve the former Supper Room (now Fire Restaurant). A simple geometrical lawn arrangement has been introduced with planted borders and hedging. The fountain and basin have been relocated to balance the symmetry of the plan.[49]

In more recent years changes that have taken place within the Mansion House have not altered the basic layout of the house to any significant extent. Most work undertaken during the second half of the twentieth century focused on maintenance and basic repairs and improving standards of accommodation for the Lord Mayor's residence, for visitors and for staff working in the house.

The Mansion House in the 21st century

There have been low points in this maintenance history. In 1976, for example, when Jim Mitchell was elected Lord Mayor, his wife Patsy described the public rooms as being in a deplorable condition. The entire building was in need of re-wiring; it was grimy from coal fires, generally neglected and badly cleaned. Curtains disintegrated when they were pulled back; heating was provided by two-bar electric fires which were totally inadequate. Basins were placed strategically around the house to catch drips from leaks in the roof. The Mitchells encouraged the renovation of the Mansion House and work eventually began, continuing right up until they left the residence in July 1977.[50] The celebration of the Dublin Millennium in 1988 led the then Lord Mayor, Carmencita Hederman, to champion a decorative renewal of the Mansion House. As part of this process, she commissioned a survey of the mayoral residence from the Irish Architectural Archive and secured the agreement of Dublin City Council's elected members that from now on no changes would be made to the residence without first consulting this survey. A decorative scheme was devised by Professor Alastair Rowan of University College Dublin and this was implemented by Ronan Boylan, Senior Executive Architect with Dublin City Council while furniture appropriate to the Mansion House was obtained. Additionally, tarmacadam covering was removed from the forecourt,

The Mansion House c.1900 showing the paved forecourt (National Library of Ireland, Laurence Collection)

MANSION HOUSE DUBLIN 1635. W.L.

revealing an early paving treatment intact underneath, in a pattern which was in place as early as 1847, when it is shown on the Ordnance Survey map of that date.

In the 1990s a multi-story car park was built on the site of the former bowling green to the rear of the Mansion House on Schoolhouse Lane. Major structural alterations were carried out to the Round Room in 1999 which included the insertion of a large ring beam to stabilize the structure.and the replacement of the roof structure and coverings. The dormer windows of the earlier roof design were not reinstated. In 2002 a commercial office block, Joshua Dawson House, was developed on the site of the former stables and yard on the south side on the Mansion House. The building was designed by Shay Cleary Architects.

Since the nineteenth century maintenance and care of the Mansion House has generally been guided by the city architect of the day and undertaken by successive city council architects, engineers, surveyors, technicians, inspectors and craftsmen who have overseen works at the house with pride, skill and enthusiasm. In the civic maintenance works team the best craftsmen were always reserved to work at the Mansion House and that tradition continues today.

A conservation and management plan for the house was prepared in 2009 by Dublin City Council's Architects Division. The plan highlights the historic significance of the house and charts its architectural history. It sets out a strategy for the care, conservation and enhancement of the house within its wider urban context. The plan includes a preliminary design for alterations and refurbishment works to greatly enhance ease of access and the presentation of the house. This would be achieved by remodelling the bar and staff offices to the rear of the main 1710 house to create a winter garden to supplement the entertainment rooms, the addition of better facilities for public receptions, making the building more universally accessible and bringing the basement of the house more fully into use. Recent recessionary times have stalled undertaking such a major refurbishment. However, having a proactive management plan for the house has meant that a number of more modest alterations and essential repair and improvement works have been planned, financed and completed in recent years.

These works have included upgrade measures resulting from an energy audit of the building. The south-facing roof of the offices to the rear of the main house accommodates solar thermal panels which provide hot water for the Lord Mayor's apartment and photovoltaic panels which generate electricity for the house. These panels were installed in 2011 as one part of a flagship energy efficiency retrofit demonstration project. The enhancement of the main reception rooms in the house has also been completed, the rooms have been redecorated, furniture has been restored and portraits cleaned and conserved. The former Supper Room (now Fire Restaurant) has been re-modelled, entrances have been rationalised, improved access has been provided to the Round Room and Oak Room, the Lord Mayor's Garden has been re-landscaped and the original forecourt plan has been reinstated.

Most importantly the dedicated and painstaking research undertaken by the City Council in these recent years has raised awareness of the unique history of the Mansion House and its significance as one of the key historic buildings in the city.

LIVING IN THE MANSION HOUSE

Una Loftus

Under a Charter issued by Charles I in 1641, the wife of the Lord Mayor of Dublin could be known as Lady, Madam or Dame. The title of Lady Mayoress was chosen and was first held in 1665 by Lady Bellingham (neé Jane Barlow) wife of Dublin's inaugural Lord Mayor, Sir Daniel Bellingham. While the Lord Mayor is elected to the office, the Lady Mayoress attains her rank by association. Accordingly, there are very few historical references to Lady Mayoresses and only one portrait known, that of Anne Overend, wife of Michael Staunton, Lord Mayor in 1847. There is also a dress by Parisien couture house Worth on display in the National Museum of Ireland at Collins Barracks, which was worn by Mary Margaret White, wife of John O'Connor, Lord Mayor in 1885.

In 1961, a decorative gold suite was made for the Lady Mayoress to wear while attending functions in the company of the Lord Mayor. This is by the Dublin silversmith J.J. McDowell, famous for 'The Happy Ring House' in O'Connell

(Right) Medallion and Tara Brooch from the
Lady Mayoress' Suite
(Joanna Travers)

(Left) The Lady Mayoress' charming parlour
(Joanna Travers)

Lady Mayoress Mary Anne Jones, wife of
William Meagher, Lord Mayor of Dublin 1885
(Dublin City Library & Archive)

Street, and consists of two separate chains, which may be worn separately or together, along with a Tara brooch, which may be worn with the chains or on its own. To one of the chains is attached a medallion having three castles imposed on a background of blue enamel and a pierced intertwined border with the motto of the city engraved. On the reverse is engraved 'Presented to Isobel McDowell [Lady Mayoress 1961–2] by J.J. McDowell.'

Acceptance of this chain was effectively the first acknowledgment that the Lady Mayoress occupies a semi-official position. This is corroborated by the annual lunch for former Lady Mayoresses, held in the Mansion House to thank them for their contribution to the city.

Today, the Lord Mayor is elected by Dublin City Council either in June or July and the term of office lasts one year. The previous Lord Mayor has a couple of days to move out, and then the new Lord Mayor can move into the Mansion House, where a spacious apartment is provided on the first floor. Of course, nowadays the Lady Mayoress might well be a man! Since 1939, Dublin has had eight women Lord Mayors and while the first two, Caitlín Bean Uí Chléirigh and Catherine Byrne, were widows the other six each had either a spouse, a partner or a brother, all of whom were glad to be male Lady Mayoresses. During the term of office, the Lord Mayor is busy with demands which often take them away from the Mansion House – council and committee meetings in City Hall, events and receptions around the city, visits around Ireland and abroad – so it is often the Lady Mayoress who sees the residence from the inside and can offer a more detailed account of what goes on there. This essay is drawn from memoirs provided by four former Lady Mayoresses: Patsy Mitchell (Jim Mitchell, 1976–7); Una Loftus (Sean D. Dublin Bay Rockall Loftus, 1995–6); Aisling Creevey (Anthony Creevey, June 2002); and Ken Byrne (Eibhlin Byrne (2008–9). They have all kindly agreed that extracts from their memoirs may be included in this essay.

All of our contributors were delighted when their spouses were elected as Lord Mayor, which meant that they would be living in the Mansion House for a year. Patsy Mitchell's husband Jim, a member of the Fine Gael party, was elected Lord Mayor in June 1976 and at the age of 29 he was the youngest Lord Mayor to date. The Mitchells were then living in Rathfarnham with their little boy Ruairi, who was just one year old, and a second child was on the way. Patsy decided that she would prefer to live in the Mansion House to be near her husband during his busy year as Lord Mayor. This caused surprise and consternation in City Hall, because no mayoral family had lived in the Mansion House for very many years – indeed there was no Lord Mayor between 1969 and 1974, when Dublin City Council was suspended for refusing to strike a rate. When the Mitchells moved into the Mansion House three weeks after the election they found that the three bedrooms and sitting room in the Lord Mayor's apartments upstairs were in good condition, well-provided with beds and furniture, however Patsy brought some tables and chairs from her own house to give it a homely feel. The rest of the residence was in a deplorable condition. The entire building needed to be re-wired, since plugs were hanging out of the walls and dangerous rusty nails were protruding from the plasterwork. The original panelling in the Oak Room was filthy, covered in years of grime and soot from coal fires, and many of the plaques carrying arms of former Lord Mayors were broken and out-of-sequence. The ladies' toilets were particularly obnoxious: a coat-hanger replaced the lavatory handle while the original stained glass windows, in a charming diamond pattern, were all missing their panes of glass, with the gaps stuffed with wads of newspaper and bits of rags. Every fireplace in the Mansion House had been closed off with large sheets of brass, which had never been cleaned and were now black and green with dirt and decay. Mirrors were cleaned only up to half-way, with the upper parts grimy and dull, and curtains disintegrated when they were pulled back. Heating was provided by two-bar electric fires sitting in the grates, totally inadequate for such large rooms. The Dining Room was especially dingy, with an old worn carpet resting on a border of lino round the edges. Basins were placed strategically around the Mansion House to catch any drips from leaks in the roof.

The Mitchells insisted that the Mansion House should be renovated and work eventually began, continuing right up until they left the residence in the following July. Quite literally, on the day they moved out, the front door was being re-painted, a job which had not been done for forty years. The ladies' toilet and kitchenette were demolished and replaced with modern facilities and the rest of the house was stripped right back to the stone and re-plastered - dust was everywhere. Inside, pipes which had corroded were replaced and outside, while missing railings were replaced. The City and County Librarian, Mairín O'Byrne, and the Curator of the Hugh Lane Gallery, Ethna Waldron, provided advice on furnishings for the rooms and selected paintings from the gallery suitable for the Mansion House. Patsy had gone exploring in the basement and found an amazing store of antique furniture which was completely covered in dust. This included superb Chinese pattern plates and a wonderful mahogany chest full of dining room silver: these were cleaned and brought back into use and are still in the Mansion House to this day. Redundant items from this store were sold and, acting on the advice of Miss O'Byrne and Miss Waldron, the proceeds were used to purchase two large chandeliers in Waterford glass for the Oak Room. Patsy also found written records of the 1880 Little Famine (which are now in the City Archives) and old guns hidden in wainscoting (which are now in the Civic Museum Collection). A new centrepiece was bought for the Dining Room table. All the fireplaces were opened up and real coal fires were lit on a regular basis - the fire in the Entrance Hall was a particularly welcoming touch for visitors. The Mitchells left the Mansion House in good decorative and working order, which was built on by their successors, with the assistance of Dublin City Council's City Architect's Department, and as it celebrates its 300th anniversary in 2015 it is in excellent condition.

Una Loftus had a personal story about the Dublin mayoralty. 'Many years ago, when I was about sixteen, I visited an aunt in Dublin. One day I was having lunch in a little restaurant and I had a conversation with a woman sharing my table. She said "Today we have a new Lord Mayor. Do you know his name?" I said that as I lived in Cootehill, a small town in Co. Cavan, he was not *my* Lord Mayor. I little thought that one day I would myself be a Lady Mayoress and live in the Mansion House.' Even though her husband Seán had spent over 30 years as a member of Dublin City Council, he never expected to be elected Lord Mayor as he was an independent and the position usually goes to the political party with the largest representation on the council. However, after the local

(Right) Lord Mayor Sean Loftus and Lady Mayoress Una Loftus with the mayoral cars for 1995 and 1996
(Family Collection)

(Below) The Loftus Family in the Lady Mayoress' Parlour
Seán and Una (*seated*) with (*left to right*) Fiona, Ruairi and Muireann
(Family Collection)

government elections of 1992, the Community Government Movement, of which he was a member, was part of the Civic Alliance and in 1995 it was their turn to hold the position. Seán was chosen to represent the C.G.M. and was duly elected Lord Mayor on Monday 3 July 1995. The couple moved into the Mansion House a week later with their younger daughter Fiona; their son Rúairí divided his time between their home in Clontarf while their daughter Muireann, who worked in Sligo, visited at weekends. Una revelled in her new position as

Lady Mayoress and found that she immediately felt at ease in the Mansion House. While larger than the average house, the mayoral residence is not so large or so grand as to be intimidating – indeed Una described it as 'a loving house.'

Aisling Creevey never expected to be Lady Mayoress either. Her husband, Anthony Creevey, a member of the Fianna Fáil party, was Lord Mayor of Dublin for the month of June 2002. This extraordinary opportunity came about because Lord Mayor Michael Mulcahy was elected to the Dáil in the General Election of May 2002 and had to give up the mayoralty as a result. As the election for a new Lord Mayor was not due until July, the Council decided to elect another Lord Mayor for the interim period, and that is how the Creeveys ended up in the Mansion House for the shortest mayoralty in history. Aisling found it to be a most extraordinary experience and the most amazing month of her life.

Ken Byrne recalls the year when 'the lady became a Lord' – his wife Eibhlin becoming only the sixth woman to be elected Lord Mayor since 1665. With three daughters, a dog and a busy professional life, Ken undertook the task of moving their closely knit and busy family to the Mansion House. As the Lord Mayor's diary begins the morning after election, family life immediately took on a new rhythm. Aisling who was in her Junior Certificate year recalls that although she frequently had an absent mother she always came back to an extended 'Mansion House family' while Lisa who was studying in Trinity and rowing for the university often crept out at dawn to train on the nearby Liffey. For Ken, days quickly took on a pattern of heading to his office in AIB Bank in the early morning, returning to the Mansion House for the 'night shift' which consisted of a series of evening engagements and welcoming guests to the residence. Like many before him, Ken quickly immersed himself in the history of this wonderful house, built c1710. He long had an interest in old buildings and observed that old houses are a little bit like old people, both deserving of tremendous care and respect. When he learned that the historic,

but threadbare, handmade carpet on the grand staircase was to be replaced by a modern weave he was determined that a more fitting alternative should be found. With some painstaking research – and the work of enlightened Irish craftsman David Geraghty - Ken succeeded in having made an exact replica of the original 100 year old carpet. Although it took a lot of effort from all concerned, Ken was satisfied that the end result was a carpet which ensured that the colours of the staircase reflect the Joshua Clarke stained glass window, just as it was always meant to.

Hospitality is a key focus of the Mansion House. For the Mitchells a particular success was the visit of Miles Humphries, Lord Mayor of Belfast, who came and stayed overnight with some members of Belfast City Council. This was a particularly important visit, in the light of the Troubles in Northern Ireland at the time. An overnight visit was also paid by the Lord Mayor and Lady Mayoress of Reykjavik, in Iceland. For these visits and for formal lunches and dinners in the Mansion House, the catering was provided by Jimmy Blowers, who was the chef with Irish Lights (as Lord Mayor, Jim Mitchell was ex-officio a Commissioner of Irish Lights). Jimmy Blowers was a wonderful chef and a lovely singer - he even helped to entertain the guests! Bord Fáilte and Dublin Tourism also provided entertainment - such as Irish dancers – and David Kennedy of Aer Lingus assisted when the Mitchells made return visits to their counterparts in Britain. Sean Loftus had three receptions for visiting heads of state – President Chiluba of Zambia; President Maarti Ahtisaari of Finland (who was later one of two international advisors brought in to inspect I.R.A. arms dumps after the Good Friday Agreement); and President Vaclav Havel of the Czech Republic. Archbishop Desmond Tutu was a welcome guest and very popular with staff when he visited the Mansion House during the Byrnes' tenure. Eibhlin and Ken Byrne regretted being in Moscow on official business when the Irish rugby team, led by their GPs son Brian O'Driscoll, visited the House after the 2009 rugby grand slam victory. Lisa and Aisling took little persuasion to represent their parents!

Ken Byrne notes that when he was growing up his late mother had attached great importance to showing hospitality: food prepared with care, served with the best china and, above all, a warm welcome. As the husband of a very busy Lord Mayor, he found that the increasing demands of his career too often made it difficult for him to be available during the day. However, he shared his wife's commitment to using the Mansion House to showcase Dublin and to bring together as many of the city's influencers as he could to rally round at a particularly difficulty time of economic challenge. The formal hospitality in the Mansion House was set at a standard that would do credit to Dublin's premier residence, silver which had lain in boxes saw the light of day once more, wonderful china bearing the Lord Mayor's crest was brought up from the basement and formal dinners were planned, with the piano in the Drawing Room filling the House with much loved music at the skilful hands of John Bennett. To Ken's great surprise many of the ordinary and extraordinary people who played key roles in Dublin's academic, religious and cultural life confessed that it was their first time to dine in Dublin's Mansion House

Apart from dignitaries, the Mansion House offers a warm welcome to Dubliners and visitors alike. The Mitchells invited groups to visit the Mansion

House and Patsy provided tea and brack on these occasions. When Sir Matt Busby and the Manchester United Football Team visited one morning, Patsy and her friend went over to Bewley's in Grafton Street and bought twenty-four bracks. The butter from the fridge was hard, but the bracks were warm and Patsy despaired of getting everything ready in time, but the team were delighted with the fare, pronouncing it delicious. The Dublin Gaelic Football Team won the All Ireland in 1976 and a civic reception was held for the team in the Mansion House. Patsy had knitted a tiny blue-and-white jersey for Rúairí and treasures a photo of him sitting in the Sam Maguire Cup and peeping out of it. Other guests included Lady Valerie Goulding, co-founder of the Central Remedial Clinic; the Archbishop of Dublin, Dr. Dermot Ryan; and Mrs. Rita Childers, widow of the late President of Ireland, Erskine Childers. Una Loftus thought that while hosting official functions to welcome dignitaries is one aspect of life in the Mansion House, she felt that it was equally important to welcome the citizens of our own city. Una particularly enjoyed taking small groups on tours of the house, sometimes in the Irish language, in which she was proficient. In one day they might have a group of school children in the morning, a visit from a new ambassador in the afternoon and a reception that night. Una remarked that in meeting the different groups, who came from all parts of the city, she became aware of the huge amount and variety of voluntary work which is being done in Dublin. 'When I hear people complain and moan about the selfishness, greed and unfriendliness of the people of Dublin, I think of all the wonderful people whom I met while I was Lady Mayoress.' Ken Byrne too remembers with particular fondness the many voluntary groups who visited the house and the headache it gave staff later to remove helium balloons from the Drawing Room ceiling in time for the next, more formal event! The Creeveys had loads of groups into the house over their month in office. Everyone from the delegation for Gay Pride week to the Retail Tyre Distributors, and a delegation of ladies from the USA crossed the threshold. The famous crooner Sonny Knowles and his Australian granddaughter were brought into the Mansion House by House Steward Ray Glynn who spotted them taking photos outside. Sonny was thrilled that the Creeveys took the time to meet his granddaughter who seemed oblivious to her granddad's reputation as a legend on the Irish cabaret circuit.

St. Patrick's Day is of course important to the Mansion House – greetings come from mayors all over the world, especially from the United States. On 17 March 1976 the newly-restored Lord Mayor's Coach was used for the first time in the parade and called early to the Mansion House to take the Mitchells to the reviewing stand in O'Connell Street, where the shamrock was solemnly blessed. Jim Mitchell was the first Lord Mayor for many years to wear the historic Great Chain, which had been a gift to Dublin from William of Orange, but this did not attract any controversy - instead, people asked if they could try it on! St. Patrick's Day ended with a grand ball in the Burlington Hotel. When Seán Loftus was Lord Mayor in 1996, the parade organisers were experimenting with the traditional layout of the event and decided that the viewing stand for City Councillors would be at City Hall. This resulted in Seán and Una boarding the Lord Mayor's Coach at Parnell Square and driving up the street to City Hall, rather than leading the parade down to the General Post Office.

As these recollections show, life in the Mansion House is always busy leaving the Lady Mayoress with little time for cooking in the private apartments. Una Loftus observed that although she always enjoyed cooking, it was not high on her agenda while in the Mansion House. Aisling Creevey noted that very often at the end of a hectic day, cooking was the last thing she wanted to do so it was not unusual to see the Lady Mayoress skipping across to Grafton Street for a McDonald's or Burger King take-away. 'Many times I would be coming back into the house when some guests would be leaving. Saying goodbyes with a McDonald's bag behind my back was a skill I acquired during my time in the house. I remember on one of our first nights in residency we ordered a Chinese take-away, which we shared with the House Steward and the photographer. We ate on the great dining room table where so many historical events took place. I quietly apologised to De Valera and Collins, as I tucked into my chow mein, but I have a feeling they would have approved.' Ken Byrne comments on his year in the Mansion House: 'We all still smile at the day when Eibhlin reminded Aisling to make sure she had a good breakfast and Aisling replied that she would happily do so....if only there was food in the house – or the occasions when one of us had to run up the stairs since the smell of a burning chicken was beginning to waft into the formal rooms because a speech had gone on too long!'

Living in the Mansion House was particularly exciting for children. Back in 1976, all the Mansion House staff doted on little Rúairí Mitchell and would take him up to St. Stephen's Green to feed the ducks. Rúairí would tease the cleaner Mrs. Grennell by pulling the plug out of the hoover as she vaccuumed. The House Steward's daughter Mary Weir would sit Rúairí on her lap as she practised the piano, and to this day, he loves to play the piano. Even though he was only two years old when his father's term of office came to an end, the little boy retained some memory of his time there. One year later, hearing his mother Patsy talk to her sister Mary on the phone, Rúairí asked: "Is that Mary from the Mansion House?" Aisling Creevey's daughter Clodagh was six in 2002 and it was difficult to maintain a sense of normality for her. Aisling began each day by getting up at around 6.30 a.m. and carrying a sleeping little girl into the car. She then 'drove the twenty miles to Naas, where we live, to my mother's house to get Clodagh ready for school.....It was so important to keep Clodagh to some sort of routine during the weekdays, as night-time and weekends were like something of a fairytale for her. When late afternoon came I hopped in my little Rover once again and dashed down the Naas dual carriageway to pick up a little person who was beside herself with excitement to get back to the *Mansion* as she called it. She was always greeted by the house staff as *Junior Lady Mayoress* or *Princess* which went down very well as you can imagine.'

It was perhaps more difficult for older children to adjust but they also enjoyed the Mansion House. Ken Byrne remarks: 'It is a matter of a family adjusting to living in what is essentially a very public environment. Evenings invariably involved public functions in the House and whatever the fare for that event it constituted our evening meal. If the girls wanted to know where their mum was, it was often a matter of following the sound of speeches coming from the Oak Room. We tried to ensure that each of our daughters had a special memory of their own to take away from our year in the Mansion House.'

Eibhlin and Ken Byrne with their children
Lisa, Aisling and Clare and Eibhlin's parents
Michael and Liz Dineen
(Family Collection)

When Aisling turned 16, the formality of the Drawing Room was for one evening turned into a cinema, thanks to a borrowed screen for a movie night. Lisa was 21 in May and friends arrived *en tuxedo* to enjoy a night of music and fun. Since Clare's friends included many Scots, her night was Hogmanay, with her friends arriving at the Mansion House to ring in the New Year in a very special way.

Of all the contributors, Patsy Mitchell had a very special experience, since her daughter Sinéad was born in the Mansion House on 30 December 1976. Only three weeks before, the Mitchells had gone to Milan on Aer Lingus's inaugural flight there. They were accompanied by Father Mulvany from the Oblates at Inchicore, who acted as the Chaplain to the Mansion House (as a boy, Jim Mitchell had been an altar server as Father Mulvany's Masses). While in Italy, the Mitchells had an audience with Pope Paul VI and the night before leaving Dublin, Patsy and her sister had been up until 4 a.m. making a long black dress for her to wear when meeting the Pope; it had a black velvet insert at the collar and black velvet cuffs. The Pope kindly asked about the coming baby and promised to offer Mass for her on Christmas Day. When Sinéad was born, a telephone call of congratulations came from the Vatican, followed by a gift of rosary beads from the Pope - the baby's second name Paula is in his honour. Dr. Paddy Hillery, President of Ireland, also telephoned with his congratulations and Taoiseach Liam Cosgrave sent his son around to the Mansion House with a lovely little dress for the baby.

There was also intense media interest, and press photographers were around to the Mansion House three hours after Sinéad was born. She was baptised in Westland Row Church and a special Mass was celebrated in the Oak Room for all the extended family, including Patsy's relations from her native Co. Galway

(Left) Lord Mayor Jim Mitchell and Lady Mayoress Patsy Mitchell, accompanied by Father Mulvany, Chaplain to the Mansion House At an audience with Pope Paul VI (Family Collection)

(Below) Jim and Patsy Mitchell with their young family, Ruairi and baby Sinéad (Family Collection)

and members of Dublin City Council. People still ask Patsy 'how is the baby who was born in the Mansion House?' The 'baby' was 25 years old in 2002, and had her 21st birthday party in her birthplace!

One of the mainstays of family life was having a much-loved pet to stay in the Mansion House, thus providing a valuable link with home. Aisling Creevey had a dog and a hamster for Clodagh while the Byrnes had a bulldog called Sam who had a wonderful effect on the very many children who visited the House. Kids just loved him and most touching of all was the bond Sam made with the many children with special needs who came to visit. Walking him in St Stephen's Green, Ken can still recall the child who shouted to his mother 'mammy, there goes a polar bear!

Like many old buildings, the Mansion House is rumoured to be haunted by a Lord Mayor whose infant daughter died in the house. The ghost is mainly detected by young people and animals and appears to frequent the old service staircase to the rear of the building, and one of the bedrooms upstairs. On one occasion, Una Loftus' son Rúairí went into the apartment's kitchen to make himself a cup of coffee. Hearing footsteps coming up the back staircase he called out that he would be in the sitting room shortly. He was amazed to find the apartment and the rest of the house empty. What is interesting is that he had not known about the ghost. Aisling Creevey notes that little Clodagh could not sleep in the famed 'haunted room'. Aisling's mother stayed in it with Clodagh one night as the large front room had no bed in it. The little girl was totally restless and was up and down all night, as she could not sleep a wink. From then on she slept on the two sofas from the apartment's sitting room pushed together so she could be close to her parents. However, Clodagh always had to fall asleep in the four poster bed. Well, every princess needs her four poster bed after all! Ken Byrne's bulldog Sam had a particular trait which would gain some notoriety. He would walk in the front door as far as the back staircase. But he would then refuse point blank to pass the backstairs even when dragged past

Sam and Friends outside the Mansion House
(Family Collection)

that point. If carried beyond the staircase he would be happy again to wander around. There is no doubt that something disturbed Sam but what it was has remained his secret.

While the Loftus family were in residence in 1995–6, the Mansion House was used as a location for the film *Michael Collins,* directed by Neil Jordan and starring Liam Neeson. Scenes were filmed in the Dining Room, and on one occasion Liam Neeson had to come down the main staircase, which was rehearsed and filmed for hours. Extensive travel is also part of the Lord Mayor's remit and Una Loftus observed that one could get accustomed to being an official visitor, having one's luggage looked after and bypassing queues. She further remarked that the one place where this was objected to, by a local who was being bypassed, was in China. An official was bringing the Lord Mayor and Lady Mayoress up a viewing tower at a beauty spot and led them to the head of the queue. He was berated by a woman whose place he was attempting to take – the Dublin visitors did not understand the exact words, but were in no doubt about the meaning! Another special event for the Loftus family was the wedding of their elder daughter Muireann. She was married in their parish church in Clontarf and the reception was held in the Mansion House Oak Room.

Christmas was a particularly lovely time for those living in the Mansion House. There was a magnificent tree in the Entrance Hall, another in the Lord Mayor's apartment and an even larger one on the forecourt outside beside the crib. This became a live animal crib during Sean Loftus's mayoralty, as arranged by the Irish Farmers' Association, and the animals were monitored by veterinary students from University College Dublin, with a voluntary donation benefiting the Lord Mayor's Fuel Fund. The animals proved to be a great attraction for children with classes from city centre schools visiting. On Christmas Eve the Loftus family attended Midnight Mass in the Pro-Cathedral and on their return they had coffee and mince pies with the House Steward in front of the fire in the Drawing Room. Christmas morning was spent visiting children's hospitals – as only really sick children were kept in hospital over the holiday period, this was a heart-breaking experience. They then returned for dinner in the Mansion House Dining Room. The Byrne family also professed Christmas as a very special time. In the run up to Christmas, a seasonal concert by tenor John McNally gave them the opportunity to thank many of those who provided the capital's essential and emergency services, while young singers from Trinity College provided the music for the city councillors' annual Christmas party. Christmas day was busy for the Lord Mayor and Lady Mayoress with hospital visits and visits to homeless and other services. That's when the mayoral granny stepped in with Liz, Eibhlin's mother setting up camp in the Mansion House kitchen from where a delicious Christmas dinner was produced with turkey rather than the swan that some early Lord Mayors might have favoured!

Patsy Mitchell found that her year in the Mansion House passed in a flash. She could have been at six or seven functions each night, but with two small children was often tied to the residence. She did judge the Rose Trials in St. Anne's Park and was asked to judge everything from Bonny Baby contests to Dog Shows. Although she had a wonderful time in the Mansion House, Patsy was glad at the end of the year to return to her own home in Rathfarnham, which had been looked after by good neighbours during her absence. She was

Sean and Una Loftus with their daughter Muireann and her bridegroom Des Gallagher In the Lady Mayoress' Parlour (Family Collection)

especially glad to have her own garden again! The very day after leaving office as Lord Mayor, Jim Mitchell was elected to Dáil Eireann, and a new and even more busy phase of their lives began. With all her new responsibilities, and with her young family to care for, Patsy now had no time to miss the Mansion House, which she describes as 'a year out of my life' but one giving her very special memories. Una Loftus left the Mansion House in tears and whenever she revisited it would walk around looking possessively at the rooms, as one might do when returning to the house of one's childhood, resenting any changes which the newcomers have made. 'It was wonderful to live in a house which was full of history. There was the sense of being part of a vibrant community, the excitement of the various events – both low-key and high-profile – and meeting such a wide variety of people.' It was true that one had very little privacy and it was very tiring – Una did not realize how exhausted she was until she went home to Clontarf. But it was a wonderful and fascinating experience which she was very glad to have had. Aisling Creevey found that leaving the Mansion House was very moving for the family. They felt very honoured to have been part of the history of such a great house – not only a house but also a home to numerous families and thoroughly enjoyed their stay even though it was so short. They grasped the challenge with both hands and packed as much into their month as they could. It was magnificent. Her advice to any future Lady Mayoress is to enjoy every second of your time there. Opportunities like this do not come by very often. Seize the day, *Carpe diem*. As Ken Byrne reflected back on his time in the Mansion House it was to the acknowledgement that as a resident of a house steeped in history you are always walking in the steps of those who have gone before. In their own small way, the Mansion House families help to ensure that the mayoral residence remains an enduring symbol of Dublin's capacity to draw from its past and embrace its future.

Front row left to right: Joe Costello,
Orla Haughey, Sinead Ahern, Jill Lacey,
Veronica Mulcahy, Miriam Ahern, Peggy Doyle,
Peggy Lynch, May MacGiolla, Margaret Bourke,
Mary O'Halloran

Back row left to right: Ken Byrne,
Fionnuala Keane, Patsy Mitchell, Veronica
Jackson, Carol Briscoe, Peggy O'Brien and
Joe Byrne Former Lady Mayoresses
photographed in January 2015

A YEAR IN THE MANSION HOUSE: 2014

Fanchea Gibson

In 2015, Dublin's Mansion House celebrates 300 years since it was purchased from Joshua Dawson for use by the Lord Mayor of Dublin. The Mansion House is the home of the Lord Mayor with a three-bedroom apartment occupying the first floor of the building. It is also the Lord Mayor's Office where he or she carries out the work of the Lord Mayor and is a public building used for functions and events. The office of the Lord Mayor of Dublin is a non-political office and the Lord Mayor represents all Dubliners.

As part of the purchase agreement in 1715, Joshua Dawson agreed to build the Oak Room for civic events. The city of Dublin and Ireland have changed dramatically since April 1715 but throughout this 300 year period the Mansion House has continued to be the official residence of the Lord Mayor of Dublin and has hosted a range of civic, national and local events and welcomed thousands of visitors through its doors. In addition, the Lord Mayor may allow the Oak Room to be used by groups, in particular community groups or charities. All use of the Mansion House must be approved by the Lord Mayor of the day in keeping with it being their official residence.

The Lord Mayor meets a wide range of people in the Mansion House during their term of office. Visiting heads of state may be welcomed with a Civic Reception, ambassadors pay a courtesy call to the Lord Mayor following their appointment to Ireland and the Lord Mayor hosts meetings on a wide range of issues in the Dining Room. Meetings throughout 2014 ranged from topics such as the directly-elected Mayor for Dublin, policing in the city centre and homelessness to a proposal for a long-distance triathlon in the city.

In 2014 the two Lord Mayors of Dublin who lived and worked in the Mansion House were Oisín Quinn and Christy Burke, with their terms of office respectively ending and beginning on 6 June 2014. Oisín, a Labour party councillor and Senior Counsel, represented the Pembroke-Rathmines ward on the City Council. Christy, an independent and full-time councillor, represented the North Inner City ward.

It is hard to convey all that happens in the Mansion House over the course of a year, but what follows is a snapshot of the many events which took place during 2014. I hope it gives a flavour of how varied and busy a year in the life of the Mansion House, Dublin can be.

Dublin's Mansion House offers a warm welcome to thousands of people each year. (Joanna Travers)

Civic Events held in 2014

Civic means 'of or relating to a city'. Civic events are held on behalf of the city so are the highest honour which can be bestowed on behalf of city government. Some of these ceremonies are held in the Mansion House and in 2014 they included a Freedom of the City ceremony, a civic reception for a visiting head of state and the holding of the Lord Mayor's Awards. At a civic event the Lord Mayor is always accompanied by his Aide-de-Camp who is a member of Dublin Fire Brigade. The Great Civic Sword, which dates from the 1390s and was the personal sword of King Henry IV, and the Great Mace of Dublin (1665) are carried by the Sword and Mace Bearers who are also members of Dublin Fire Brigade and form the ceremonial party.

Months of preparation go into the organising of civic events and involves co-operation with other City Council Departments, in particular Chief Executive's Department, the Media Relations Department, Dublin City Library & Archives, International Relations and Dublin Fire Brigade. Advance preparations include invites and RSVPs, booklets, gifts, preparation of the venue and ensuring the Mansion House is looking its best. A cleaning programme for the big day includes everything down to cleaning the brass rails which hold the red carpet in place on the steps.

Fr. Peter McVerry S.J. and Brian O'Driscoll Received the Freedom of Dublin on 22 March 2014

Freedom of the City 2014

On 22 March, Fr. Peter McVerry SJ and Brian O'Driscoll were the 77th and 78th persons to be conferred with the Honorary Freedom of Dublin City. This is the highest honour that the city of Dublin can bestow on individuals who have made a major contribution to the life of Dublin city or to honour important international visitors. To put this in context previous recipients include Irish politician Charles S. Parnell, tenor John McCormack, US Presidents John F. Kennedy and Bill Clinton, Pope John Paul II, political leaders Nelson Mandela and Aung San Suu Kyi and local sporting heroes Stephen Roche and Ronnie Delany. Fr. Peter and Brian were chosen by Lord Mayor Oisín Quinn and their selection was ratified by the City Council at the council meeting of 4 November 2013. Fr. Peter was chosen for his 30 years of tireless work and campaigning for the rights of Dublin's young homeless. Brian is widely acclaimed as Ireland's best ever rugby union player and is also an active supporter of children's charities.

The date for the ceremony was set for 22 March and after months of work behind the scenes the red carpet was rolled out on the steps of the Mansion House and Fr. Peter and Brian arrived at 6pm. After the press conference, photo call and some private time with the Lord Mayor, the ceremonial party processed into the Round Room at the Mansion House for the formal ceremony. The ceremony is an official City Council meeting and guests include the members of Dublin City Council and invited guests of the two recipients. During the ceremony the Lord Mayor outlined the reasons for the honour and invited both men to sign the Roll of Honorary Freedom where their signatures joined those of the previous 76 recipients.

Lord Mayor's Awards

On 4 February, The Lord Mayor's Awards were held at the Mansion House and the Round Room at the Mansion House. These awards were established in 1989 to acknowledge and congratulate individuals and groups who have made

Containers for freedom scrolls presented to Fr. Peter McVerry S.J. and Brian O'Driscoll

a special contribution to Dublin. The choice of recipients is personal to the Lord Mayor of the day and covers a range of areas including sport, the arts and social justice and is also a mix of recipients from the well-known to someone who has quietly done work in their local community. Following a photo call and private reception in the Mansion House, the recipients proceeded into the Round Room at the Mansion House for the awards ceremony and gala dinner. Recipients in 2014 were:

- Paddy Cosgrave, Organiser of Dublin Web Summit
- Jim Gavin, Dublin Senior Football Manager – All Ireland Winners in 2013
- Ranelagh Arts Festival
- One Young World – the Dublin bid team
- St. Andrew's Resource Centre
- Dil Wickremasinghe – social justice, mental health broadcaster and activist

It is a wonderful evening where recipients are publicly acknowledged for their work and contribution to the city of Dublin.

Civic Reception in honour of President of Republic of Mozambique

Civic Receptions are held by the Lord Mayor for visiting heads of state or other international dignitaries. On 5 June the Lord Mayor hosted a Civic Reception in honour of HE Mr. Armando Emílio Guebuza, President of the Republic of

H.E. Mr. Armando Emilio Guebuza, President of the Republic of Mozambique, signing the Visitors' Book in the Mansion House while Lord Mayor Oisin Quinn looks on (Joanna Travers)

Mozambique. The Lord Mayor and President had a private meeting in the Lady Mayoress Parlour before the ceremonial procession brought them to the Oak Room where they both spoke about the relationship between Ireland and Mozambique. There was an exchange of gifts with an engraved Dublin Crystal Vase being presented to President Guebuza and the Lord Mayor receiving a piece of artwork by Mozambican artist Dimande. The President was very interested in the history of the Mansion House and in particular the Oak Room where meetings of the Executive Council of the first Dáil Eireann here held.

The organisation of Civic Receptions is done in cooperation with the Department of Foreign Affairs and Trade who organise the State Visit of a visiting dignitary.

Visit of Canadian Astronaut Chris Hadfield
The first international visitor to the Mansion House in 2014 arrived on Friday 10 January. Canadian astronaut Chris Hadfield had been awarded a Lord Mayor's Award in 2013 by former Lord Mayor Naoise Ó Muirí for highlighting the work on the International Space Station through social media and being the first person to tweet from outer space *as Gaeilge*. As Chris had literally just come back to earth at the time of the ceremony in May 2013, his attendance to formally sign the Roll of Honour was delayed until January 2014. Chris arrived at the Mansion House with his wife Helene and during the photo call took a great interest in the Civic Sword. During the ceremony he signed the Roll of Honour for the Lord Mayor's Awards and spoke to the attendees about his time in space and his love of Ireland. He topped off the morning accompanying himself on the House Steward's guitar as he sang Christy Moore's *Ride On* and finished off with a pint of Guinness from the Mansion House bar.

Lying in Repose of former Taoiseach Albert Reynolds
In the early morning of Thursday 21 August, a phone call was received from the Department of An Taoiseach for the use of the Oak Room for the lying in repose of former Taoiseach the late Albert Reynolds, a request which was quickly granted by the Lord Mayor. Preparatory work began immediately with meetings of all involved – staff from the Mansion House, Department of An Taoiseach, OPW, An Garda Síochána, Defence Forces, RTÉ and the Funeral Director. All had their own individual responsibilities. The Mansion House staff prepared the residence and Oak Room for the event and helped manage the public on the day. The Department of An Taoiseach looked after the State funeral as a whole and remained as a presence in the Oak Room, the OPW took responsibility for the staffing of the Mansion House forecourt and the organising of the queuing system, An Garda Síochána managed any traffic concerns and the Defence Forces provided the ceremonial Pall Bearer party. Assistance was also received from Dublin City Council's Cleansing Unit who prioritised Dawson Street for cleaning that morning and the Railway Procurement Agency who ceased all noisy Luas Cross City works for the duration of the event. While it would be a formal event, it was also a very personal family funeral and it was important to retain that balance and ensure the family had time in private. The Lying in Repose took place on Saturday 23 August and over 5,000 members of the public filed past the coffin which was laid out in the Oak Room.

(Previous page) Canadian astronaut Chris Hadfield in the Mansion House Oak Room (Joanna Travers)

Annual Events

There are a number of functions which are held on an annual basis in the Mansion House.

Election of the Lord Mayor of Dublin

The changeover of Lord Mayor took place on 6 June 2014. Due to the local elections being held on 23 May, the date of the annual general meeting of Dublin City Council was held on a Friday in early June as it had to be held on the 14th day after polling day. Lord Mayor Oisín Quinn spent time during the previous week tidying out personal belongings from the Lord Mayor's Apartment and his office. On the morning of 6 June, the cleaning staff moved into the office and gave it a good turn-out in anticipation of its new occupant. Lunch is a long-standing tradition with all staff sitting down to fish & chips with the outgoing Lord Mayor. He was presented with an album containing photos from some of the events throughout the term of office and exchanged memories from what was a busy year. At 4pm the Lord Mayor left the Mansion House and travelled to City Hall for the Annual General Meeting of the City Council where a new Lord Mayor was elected. At about 8pm the newly elected Lord Mayor Christy Burke arrived at the Mansion House and received the keys from outgoing Lord Mayor Oisín Quinn. He was introduced to all staff, was invited to sign the Visitors' Book and then moved into the Oak Room for a few speeches and a reception.

On the following Monday, 9 June, all staff gathered in the Drawing Room to chat to the new Lord Mayor and outline their roles within the office and hear about his aims and initiatives for his year in office. It is a time of new beginnings and is a strange day for staff as they get to know their new boss for the next year.

St. Patrick's Festival

St. Patrick's weekend in the middle of March is a very busy time in the Mansion House diary. The house is used extensively as part of the St. Patrick's Day celebrations and in 2014 these included:

Weekend	The Mansion House was lit in green as part of the *Green your City* initiative joining buildings all around the world which went green.
15th March	Reception for international media in Dublin for St. Patrick's Festival
16th March	Meeting point for the Lord Mayor's 5 Alive Challenge Team who took part in the St. Patrick's Festival 5k race around the streets of Georgian Dublin. Welcome Reception for bands taking part in St. Patrick's Festival Parade
17th March	Awards ceremony for pageant and marching bands in St. Patrick's Festival Parade

As part of these celebrations German Marching Band *Guggemusik* entertained the crowds outside the Mansion House with their vibrant brass music before the Awards Ceremony.

(Overleaf) Outgoing Lord Mayor Oisin Quinn (*left*) with incoming Lord Mayor Christy Burke at the Mansion House, 6 June 2014 (Joanna Travers)

Lord Mayor's Coach

The Lord Mayor's Coach is used on two occasions each year – during the St. Patrick's Day Parade and on early August when it brings the Lord Mayor and his family to the opening day of the Dublin Horse Show in the Royal Dublin Society (RDS). The coach is pulled by four horses and on 6th August 2014 it pulled onto the forecourt for half an hour. It attracts lots of attention with numerous photos being taken, including an annual staff photo.

Lord Mayor Oisin Quinn in the historic Lord Mayor's Coach during the St. Patrick's Day Parade
(Joanna Travers)

Culture Night and Open House

The Mansion House takes part in the annual Culture Night and Irish Architecture Foundation's Open House initiatives. The Mansion House offers tours and former Lord Mayors and Lady Mayoresses come back to the Mansion House to tell the history of the House and impart some of their own experiences of living in Dublin's premier address. During their terms of office Lord Mayors are told a great many stories about the Mansion House and some go on to become 'urban legends'. Unfortunately in 2014, during a review of old documents from the basement, we discovered a few of our old favourite stories were not as factual as previously thought! Two favourite tales which had to be amended were that the chandeliers in the Oak Room had not come from the Metropole Hotel and the grand piano in the Drawing Room didn't have a connection with Irish tenor John Count McCormack!

Dublin: One City One Book

A very popular event in the Mansion House diary, the launch of the 2014 Dublin: One City One Book project took place on 25 March. The 2014 Book was *If ever you go, A Map of Dublin in Poetry & Song* and invited people to explore the streets of Dublin through the poems and songs it has inspired down the ages. The launch was organised by Dublin City Public Libraries and this year's distinguished guests included Brendan Kennelly who recited *Raglan Road* and John Sheehan of The Dubliners who delighted the guests, and staff, with his beautiful playing of the tin whistle. John is a very popular guest with the staff of the Mansion House as he usually has a tin whistle in his pocket and can be called upon to play some tunes!

John McCormack Society

One of the traditional annual events to take place in the Mansion House is a concert by the John McCormack Society of Ireland, which celebrates the work-famous Irish tenor, and in 2014 it was held on 28 March. There is an association between John McCormack and the Mansion House as his yellow piano was kept in the Dining Room for many years. Today a Petrov Grand Piano on loan from the Dublin Institute of Technology is used to accompany the singers on the night to remember a singer who still today is the comparison point for all tenors.

Anzac Day

25 April is the anniversary of the start of the Battle of Gallipoli during World War I and is marked as 'Anzac Day' remembering those from Australia and New Zealand who died during the battle. In Dublin the Lord Mayor travels to Grangegorman Military Cemetery for the Dawn Service and then welcomes representatives of the Australian and New Zealand embassies and their guests to the Mansion House for a reception that evening.

Lord Mayor's Charity Ball

Lord Mayor Christy Burke held a Charity Ball on 24 October 2014 to raise money for three great charities – The Capuchin Day Centre, Inner City Helping Homeless and the Irish Hospice Foundation. The Ball was sponsored by The Conference & Events Venue at The Mansion House meaning that all monies raised went directly to the three charities. The Lord Mayor's Ball dates back to 1715 when it took place in the Oak Room of the Mansion House on St. Stephen's night and the principal invited guests were the city's 24 Aldermen and their wives.

It has been held on and off in various locations throughout the city over the years but in 2013 was revived by Lord Mayor Naoise Ó Muirí back in the Mansion House. In 2014 the MC on the night was Aonghus McAnally with Karen & the Dolans providing the music. The Lord Mayor took his turn on lead

mic singing the Joe Dolan version of *Unchained Melody*. Next up was Aonghus McAnally who wowed the crowd with lead guitar and vocal renditions of Status Quo's *Rockin' all over the World* and Thin Lizzy's *Whiskey in the Jar*. A total of €51,819 was raised from the evening which was split evenly between the three charities.

International IMPAC Dublin Literary Award announcement

12 June saw the International IMPAC Dublin Literary Award announcement held at lunchtime in the Round Room at the Mansion House. This is presented for a novel in English or for one translated into that language and is the most valuable international award for a single work of literature. The Mansion House welcomed the winner, Juan Gabriel Vásquez, who won for his book *The Sound of Things Falling*. A pre-announcement reception was held in the Mansion House before the ceremonial party moved into the Round Room for the announcement.

Bloomsday Messenger Bike Rally

On 13 June, three days before Bloomsday, the Lord Mayor welcomed the Bloomsday Messenger Bike Rally party who gather on the steps of the Mansion House for a photo with the Lord Mayor and a rendition of Molly Malone before setting off from the Mansion House by bike.

(Above) Lord Mayor Christy Burke reviews his speech before the Lord Mayor's Ball at the Mansion House, 24 October 2014 (Joanna Travers)

(Right) Lord Mayor Christy Burke sending off the Bloomsday Bike Rally, 13 June 2014 (Joanna Travers)

(Overleaf) The Mansion House weathering a snowstorm, Christmas 2010 (Joanna Travers)

Dublin Marathon Breakfast

Dublin City Council and the Lord Mayor are very proud to support the SSE Airtricity Dublin City Marathon which takes place annually on the October Bank Holiday Monday. Inaugurated in 1980, the Marathon was the brainchild of Dublin Corporation's former Public Relations Officer Noel Carroll, who was one of Ireland's leading athletes and the City Council continues to support it to this day. The Lord Mayor hosted a Breakfast for VIPs attending the Marathon who come to the Mansion House after waving off the runners at the start line. The timeframe was adjusted slightly on the day on 27th October as word came through that Patrick Monahan was leading the wheelchair race and looking like finishing in under 2 hours. So the guests ate a little quicker, the speeches were a little shorter and all were back at the finish line to see Patrick coming over the finish line in a Dublin course record of 01:52:43.

Christmas at the Mansion House

Live Animal Crib

Christmas really starts at the Mansion House with the opening of the Live Animal Crib on the forecourt. This longstanding tradition shows the traditional nativity scene in a log cabin with live donkey, sheep and goat. The crib is a joint initiative of Dublin City Council and the Irish Farmers' Association (IFA) with the City Council's Housing Department building the crib and the IFA supplying and caring for the animals. Launched on the 9th December, the crib was formally opened by Lord Mayor Christy Burke and IFA President Eddie Downey and blessed by Fr. John Gilligan of St. Andrew's Church in Westland Row.

Lucan Gospel Choir got everyone into the Christmas mood but the stars of the show were the three year old little angels who come from St. Joseph's Nursery School. They treated us to five songs complete with actions and featured heavily in the photo sections of the following day's newspapers! We at the Mansion House were delighted that a photo of a little angel from 2010 was chosen to be the 2014 Christmas stamp by An Post. Admission to the crib is free and donations to the Mansion House Fuel Fund, the Lord Mayor's charity which assist those in need in Dublin, are welcome.

On Saturdays 13 and 20 December the afternoons at the crib were filled with song as choirs came and gave of their time freely to entertain visitors to the Live Animal Crib. It really brought a Christmas cheer to Dawson Street.

The Mansion House Fuel Fund

The Mansion House Fuel Fund is the Lord Mayor's only personal charity and was set up by Sir John Arnott in 1891. It was originally established to assist the needy during a particularly hard winter and continues to distribute cash grants through a number of Charitable Societies including St. Vincent de Paul and Dublin Simon.

The Lord Mayor also holds a Christmas Concert for the Mansion House Fuel Fund and on Sunday 21 December he welcomed 500 people to the Round Room where entertainment was provided by the Band of An Garda Síochána.

Bobbi and Lily, participants in The Live
Animal Crib
(Joanna Travers)

Christmas Day

Christmas Day saw Lord Mayor Christy Burke travelling to visit children in hospital in both Temple Street University Hospital and Our Lady's Children's Hospital, Crumlin. He also visited A&E staff in the Mater Hospital before heading to the dinner for the homeless in the Royal Dublin Society. He returned to the Mansion House that afternoon to celebrate Christmas with his family for dinner in the Dining Room.

Chanukah Celebrations

We are always happy to welcome the Dublin Jewish Community to the Mansion House every December for their annual Chanukah Celebrations. On 16th December Rabbi Zalman Lent led the Jewish Community in the celebrations.

There have been two Jewish residents of the Mansion House in recent years with Bob Briscoe (1956-7 and 1961-2) and his son Ben Briscoe (1988-9) both being Lord Mayors of Dublin.

Lord Mayor Christy Burke with the 'Wran Boys'
In the Mansion House Drawing Room
17 December 2014
(Joanna Travers)

The Wran Boys

Another Irish tradition was celebrated early on 17 December at the Mansion House when the Wran Boys came to visit the Lord Mayor to launch their planned events which are held in Sandymount on St. Stephen's Day. Their colourful costumes and masks definitely liven up the Mansion House and the Lord Mayor joined in a number of tunes.

Guests received at the Mansion House

International visitors

The Mansion House welcomes visitors from all over the world every year. Groups welcomed included those in Dublin for Dublin Web Summit and other international conferences. In 2014 we welcomed visitors from the UK, USA, Canada, Mexico, Holland, France, Brazil, China, India, Thailand, Turkey, Georgia, Portugal and Mozambique. Dignitaries included the Mayor of Boston Martin J. Walsh and the Governor of Bangkok M.R. Sukhumbhand Paribatra.

The Lord Mayor hosted a Welcome Reception for attendees at the Mexico Dublin Business Conference in the Mansion House on 30 April. The Conference was a joint venture of Dublin City Council, the Mexican Embassy in Ireland and the Department of Foreign Affairs and Trade and showcased Dublin as a gateway to Europe to business and education leaders from Mexico.

In December, the Lord Mayor welcomed Mayors and senior delegates to the Mansion House. They were attending the meeting of the UCEU (Union of Capital Cities of the European Union) which was hosted by Dublin in 2014. The UCEU provides a platform for the Capital Cities of Europe to share, create dialogue and shape policy.

The Lord Mayor and the Mayor of Tbilisi, Georgia met on 10th December to sign a Memorandum of Understanding between the two cities to strengthen co-operation between them.

On the 16th December the Lord Mayor of London Andrew Yarrow was welcomed to the Mansion House for a courtesy call and meeting. Earlier in 2014 the Lord Mayor of Dublin was welcomed to the Mansion House in London, so this meeting further strengthened the growing relationship between the two cites.

The Mansion House has a close relationship with the many Embassies located in Dublin city. Following the election of the Lord Mayor, all Ambassadors pay a courtesy call on the Lord Mayor, as first citizen of the city. The Lord Mayor and Dublin City Council are supportive of events organised by the embassies and some of these are held in the Mansion House including National Day Receptions.

The Mexican Embassy also holds the closing event of their Cultural and Gastronomic Festival in the Oak Room and in 2014 the Mexican restaurants of Dublin vied for the title of 'Best Enchilada' – won by our Dawson Street neighbours *Little Ass Burrito*.

The partners of ambassadors resident in Ireland organise the annual International Charity Bazaar and raise monies for various charities. Their Award presentation was held in the Oak Room on 16 December.

Navy Ships

One of the more unusual roles of the Lord Mayor is that he is Honorary Admiral of Dublin Port. This dates from 1582 when the title was conferred on the then Mayor of Dublin by Queen Elizabeth I of England. The Mayor was to have jurisdiction as Admiral over the coastline from Arklow to Co. Meath and was entitled to receive customs duties payable to the city for goods unloaded within this area. Today, as part of this role, the Lord Mayor receives captains from naval ships visiting the city at the Mansion House where they pay a courtesy call to him as Honorary Admiral of Dublin Port.

Sporting Guests

The Lord Mayor holds receptions for sporting organisations and teams who have achieved success in their sporting fields. In 2014 we welcomed:

* St. Patrick's Athletic Football Club who won FAI Ford Cup Senior Final
* Raheny United Ladies Soccer Team, winners of the 2014 Women's FAI Cup
* "All Stars" U-14 basketball team drawn from various clubs in Dublin who won an International basketball tournament in Wanze, Belgium.
* The Irish Homeless World Cup Street Soccer Team prior to their departure for the World Cup in Chile

- Dublin Ladies Gaelic Football team after they reached the All-Ireland Final
- FAI Women's U19 Team who reached the semi-finals of the UEFA Women's Under 19 championships
- Gabrielle McDonald who was the first Irish person to complete her FIA Top Fuel Dragster licence. FIA is drag racing's version of Formula 1.
- Tony Mangan who completed his run around the world by completing the Dublin Marathon 2014. Tony visited the Mansion House and met with the Lord Mayor on 21 November.
- The participants in the 2014 Lord Mayor's 5 Alive Challenge – people who took up the Lord Mayor's challenge to get fit in 2014 and took part in five of Dublin's road races.
- International Martial Arts Ambassadors
- Irish Blackball Association (Pool) members who represented Ireland at the World Championships in October winning a range of medals including a Team Gold Medal in the Senior Blackball event.

Lord Mayor Christy Burke poses with a model elephant at the Mansion House
(Joanna Travers)

Events held during 2014

Anyone can request to use the Oak Room of the Mansion House. Permission is granted by the Lord Mayor and priority is given to local groups and charitable organisations. Some very interesting and special events are held in the House.

Jameson Dublin International Film Festival

On 14 February the Lord Mayor welcomed a range of Irish filmmakers and celebrated their achievements at the 2014 Jameson Dublin International Film Festival. On 18 February the Deputy Lord Mayor Henry Upton, representing the Lord Mayor, welcomed Richard Dreyfuss to the Mansion House for a press conference in the Oak Room. Joining Richard were his wife Svetlana Erokhin and Irish Director Jim Sheridan.

Imagine Dublin 2030

7 May saw a hundred children descend on the Mansion House to view the entries received as part of the Lord Mayor's *Imagine Dublin 2030* initiative. The Lord Mayor asked 2nd 3rd and 4th class children to say via drawing or poetry what they thought Dublin would be like in 2030. All the entries were put on a usb disk and buried in a time capsule in the Lord Mayor's Garden to be re-opened by a future Lord Mayor in 2030.

Senior Citizens Tea Dance

A wide range of citizens of the city visit the Mansion House and on 31 March we welcomed the senior citizens and volunteers from Marino for an Afternoon Tea Dance. Pat Lee on piano got the afternoon going and there was a long line of willing singers waiting to entertain. These days always remind staff how Dubliners appreciate being in the Mansion House and how they recognise it as one of the special buildings in the city.

Inland Waterways

On 8 May the Lord Mayor hosted a group of volunteers from Inland Waterways who clean up the Canals on an ongoing basis. One of the main organisers of the Group is Mick Kinahan who for many years looked after the Lord Mayor's Coach.

Former Lord Mayors & Lady Mayoresses

On 27 May, the Lord Mayor invited former Lord Mayors and Lady Mayoresses to the Mansion House. The former residents of the Mansion House love coming back into the House and exchange stories and comments from their times living on Dawson Street. This event was tinged with sadness due the recent death of former Lady Mayoress Úna Loftus who had passed away a short time before. Úna was a regular visitor to the Mansion House and gave such engaging and personal tours to the public on Culture Night and Open House days giving the history of the house but also her recollections from living in the Mansion House.

Charities

A range of charities use the Mansion House to launch and promote their work. The Lord Mayor and Mansion House staff got into the spirit of the Ice Bucket Challenge in aid of Motor Neurone disease and Light it up Gold Children's Cancer. The Dublin Society for Prevention of Cruelty to Animals are regular visitors and launch their Christmas appeal at the Mansion House each year. In 2014 the Lord Mayor was upstaged by dogs Ruby, Amber and MJ who charmed their way through the photo shoot.

Elephants!

After the birth of three baby elephants in Dublin Zoo during the summer of 2014, October was declared the month of the Elephants in Dublin city. As part of the festivities a photo call was arranged at the Mansion House to promote the Elephant Trail around the City Centre. The star turn was a giant inflatable elephant which caused much talk from passersby. The quickest reaction was a Dublin Bus tour guide who, without knowing about the photo call, was overheard saying *'On the right is the Mansion House, home of the Lord Mayor and an Elephant!'*

Launches

The Oak Room is a popular venue for launches with 46 held during 2014. These launches included books, annual reports and awareness campaigns for a number charities, film and theatre festival launches, the re-launch of the *Dublin Gazette* newspaper, press launches of major events for Dublin, a new Irish language website *tuairisc.ie* and the 2014 GAA Football Championship.

With the Decade of Commemorations underway there were a number of historical Book launches. Of special meaning to the Mansion House was the launch of Kathleen McKenna's *A Dáil Girl's Revolutionary Recollections* which took place on 1 October. Carefully put together by her daughter Teresa Napoli, this book contains the memoirs of Kathleen McKenna who from 1919 worked as private secretary to Arthur Griffith and other Ministers of the Irish Free State Government. She worked in the Mansion House and she describes where

Margaret McCann of the Mansion House Staff Interviewed by Ray D'Arcy then of TodayFM about her participation in the 'Shave or Dye' campaign
(Joanna Travers)

she worked, the staff of the Mansion House and the famous visitors including Michael Collins. It was very appropriate that the House welcomed Kathleen's daughter Teresa back to launch her mother's memoirs.

Shave or Dye – record breakers!
On 21 February there was great excitement in the Mansion House as staff member, Margaret McCann, joined with 178 others to shave her head to raise money for the Irish Cancer Society as part of Today fm's Shave or Dye campaign. The shaving of heads took place in the Round Room at the Mansion House with the group photo on the Mansion House forecourt immediately afterwards. Guinness World Record Adjudicator, Anna Orford, confirmed the World Record for the Most Heads Shaved Simultaneously had been broken with a new record of 179!

Dublin Fire Brigade Log Book
A Dublin Fire Brigade Log book dating from Easter Week in 1916 was purchased by Dublin City Library & Archive. This fascinating book documents the work done by the Fire Brigade during the Easter Rising and gives the names and locations of those who were injured. On 20th November the book was brought to the Mansion House for a photo call.

World Aids Day
On 1 December, the Mansion House joined other cities worldwide to highlight the continued existence of HIV and AIDS. The Mansion House was lit in red and an event was held in the Oak Room to launch the booklet *HIV – Our Responsibilities.*

Emergency Summit on Homelessness

Following the death of Jonathan Corrie on the streets of Dublin, the Lord Mayor Christy Burke called an emergency summit of those who work with the homeless on 5 December. Representatives from Dublin City Council, Dublin Region Homeless Executive, Government Departments and groups who work with the homeless attended and outlined concerns and actions required to deal with the homeless crisis in Dublin.

Dublin Fire Brigade

Dublin Fire Brigade came to visit on 11 December when they awarded the prizes for their Fire Safety Week competition. This competition is held by Dublin Fire Brigade and school children paint pictures to highlight the dangers of fire in the home. The winners feature in the 2015 Dublin Fire Brigade Fire Safety Calendar and will serve as an ongoing reminder throughout 2015 of the importance of Fire Safety. As well as the presentation of prizes to the winners, they all got to sit into a Dublin Fire Brigade Fire Engine which was parked on the forecourt for the morning.

Pat Kenny Radio Show

On 19 December the Mansion House welcomed Newstalk and broadcaster Pat Kenny for their final broadcast before Christmas. The Oak Room was set up for the radio broadcast with invited guests seated and enjoying the hospitality. Guests included upcoming boyband Hometown, The Swing Cats, actor Rory Cowan, X Factor's Louis Walsh, rugby analyst Brent Pope, chef Neven Maguire and Boxing World Champion Andy Lee.

Working in the Mansion House

Staff

The Mansion House is quite a unique place to work and every day is different. There is a permanent staff of eleven people in the House consisting of five office staff, four house staff and two drivers. The office staff run the Office of the Lord Mayor and co-ordinate the Lord Mayor's diary, organise functions and manage the granting of the Oak Room. The House Stewards are the first to greet guests at the door and look after the Lord Mayor's guests and assist those using the Oak Room while the two cleaners keep the House in top condition.

In addition there is a lot of assistance given by other staff of the City Council including the Conservation Section of the Architects Department, City Archivist, Civic Maintenance and Electrical Division.

The daily running of the Mansion House must always be flexible as we have learned to adapt to daily changes in planning. The Lord Mayor can get called away on urgent business and a representative must be arranged on short notice, visitors can arrive early ...... or late, the political climate can mean protests outside the Mansion House leading to changes in access to the House. But through the year, the staff continued to work with circumstances outside their control and smile while delivering the work of the Mansion House.

Upkeep of the Mansion House

There is ongoing discussion regarding the Mansion House when it comes to the conservation of the House. It is a busy working house with hundreds of visitors daily. It is the Lord Mayor's working office and their home. It is an important and historic civic building but not a museum. Therefore it is critical that there is a balance between the conservation and decoration of the Mansion House and the requirements of a busy 21st century working building. Overall responsibility for the Mansion House lies with Dublin City Council's Chief Executive's Department with assistance and guidance from Dublin City Architect's Department's Conservation Section.

Annual maintenance works

In 2014 the Mansion House closed from 16 June while the annual refurbishment programme got underway. This is always a strange period during the year in the Mansion House as the bustle of visitors and groups using the Oak Room changes for the quieter noises of painters, carpenters and inspections.

Every year a different project is prioritised and in 2014 the Lady Mayoress' Parlour was re-decorated. Always known as "The Blue Room", due to a previous painting scheme, it was returned from magnolia to a beautiful blue colour. The shade of blue to be used was debated as historic paint colours were weighed against the daily use of the room as the main room for photographs of the Lord Mayor and guests.

The exterior of the Mansion House was overdue for painting and also major repair work to the façade. To ensure the Mansion House looks its best for 2015, this work was also carried out during the summer of 2014. All painting work

The Lady Mayoress' Parlour at the Mansion House following refurbishment, Summer 2014 (Joanna Travers)

was carried out by Dublin City Council staff based in the Housing Department. It was a great success with numerous phone calls to the Lord Mayor's Office saying how wonderful the Mansion House looked and asking what colour was used. For those interested it is Dulux All Seasons Cloud!

Paintings

The paintings which hang in the Lady Mayoress Parlour are on loan from Dublin City Gallery the Hugh Lane. Due to the refurbishment of the Parlour, the paintings which were hanging in the room were returned to Dublin City Gallery the Hugh Lane on 17 June. Lord Mayor Christy Burke visited the Gallery to choose a new selection of paintings for the room and these were re-hung on 17 September 2014. The paintings hung in the Lady Mayoress's Parlour in September are:

- Winetavern Street (1934) by Harry Kernoff
- Coles Lane, Dublin (late 1930's / early 1940's) by Fergus O'Ryan
- Weaver Square by Lizzie Stephens
- Sheep Shearing (1901) by Dermod O'Brien
- Bring Home the Seaweed (1944) by Charles Lamb

Charles Stewart Parnell

There are many valuable portraits in the Mansion House which need specialist care. On 24 March the portrait of Charles Stewart Parnell by Sir Thomas Alfred Jones and dating from 1892 was taken off-site from the Oak Room for restoration. This portrait is one of the key portraits in the Mansion House and features in all Mansion House Tours. His absence was missed in the Oak Room and resulted in a few embarrassed faces as Tour Guides started to give the history of the portrait, while waving their hands in its 'direction', only to look around mid-way through their speech to find it missing! The portrait was re-hung in the Mansion House on 4 June.

Bookcase

One of the first features seen by visiting guests is the beautiful Georgian mahogany breakfront bookcase in the Entrance Hall. This bookcase was formerly in the Irish House of Lords, which was abolished in 1801 and was situated in what is now Bank of Ireland College Green. There is a plaque on the bookcase inscribed with *"Bookcase formerly in the Irish House of Lords presented to the Irish Home Rule League by Michael Henry Esq. MP."* The bookcase was also repaired in 2014 with repair work to the doors, glass and wood. It now displays gifts given to Lord Mayors by visiting dignitaries.

Emergency works

The heavy rainfall in early 2014 resulted in water coming in the Oak Room roof. After an emergency dash to a local hardware store, buckets were placed in strategic locations. The City Architect's Department then arranged for an inspection and repair of the roof.

The roof needs regular inspections to check that drains and gullies aren't blocked by debris. However access to the roof is reduced in springtime when

The Supper Room in its incarnation
as Fire Restaurant.
(Conor McCabe)

a pair of seagulls take up residence beside the old chimney pots to raise their family. They don't appreciate visitors so checks to the roof are reduced during this timeframe!

Conclusion

The Mansion House has survived as the home of the Lord Mayor for three centuries. Life in Dublin has changed dramatically in this time from being the second city of the British Empire through the 1916 Rising, the War of Independence and Civil War, finally emerging as the capital of an independent Ireland. Through all this time the Mansion House has been a key venue in the city and has witnessed much history. We hope it will continue to fulfil this role for another 300 years.

So to finish, here's 2014 in the Mansion House in numbers:

- Over 26,000 visitors
- 21,829 photographs
- 6,000 teabags
- 350 meetings
- 320 litres of milk
- 40 Courtesy Calls
- 15 Portraits from the Civic Collection
- 11 Staff
- 5 Civic Events
- 4 Seagulls
- 2 Lord Mayors
- 1 Mansion House

Overleaf: Tea-time at the Mansion House -
the china cups bear the Lord Mayor's Arms
(Joanna Travers)

APPENDIX 1: A LIST OF DUBLIN CITY ARCHITECTS

Researched by Andrew O'Brien, Dublin City Archives

John Semple – City Architect 1824 to 1841
Hugh Byrne – City Architect 1842 to 1869
John S. Butler – City Architect 1869 to 1878
1879 - Vacant
Daniel Freeman – City Architect 1880 to 1893
Charles J. McCarthy – City Architect 1894 to 1921
Horace T. O'Rourke – City Architect 1922 to 1945
1946 - Vacant
Conor Mac Fhionnlaoich – City Architect 1947 to 1959
Daithi Hanly – City Architect 1960 to 1965
T. Randall – City Architect 1966 to 1969
T. Randall – Chief Civic & Amenities Architect (Acting) 1970 to 1973
Housing Architect – Vacant 1970 to 1974
Chief Civic & Amenities Architect – Vacant 1974
C. Dardis – Chief Civic & Amenities Architect 1975 to 1989
J.F. Maguire – Chief Housing Architect 1975 to 1985
J. McDaid – Chief Housing Architect 1986 to 1988
Chief Housing Architect – Vacant 1989
C. Dardis – City Architect 1990 - 1993
C. Garvey – City Architect (Acting) 1994
Jim Barrett – City Architect 1995 – 2006
Ali Grehan – City Architect 2007 – 2015

APPENDIX 2: STAFF OF THE MANSION HOUSE 2014–5

Fanchea Gibson

(Left) Present and former managers of the Mansion House
Left to right: John Bergin, Fanchea Gibson, Clare Ennis, Ailish Smyth, Hugh Fahey

Lord Mayor Christy Burke with his staff before the Lord Mayor's Ball
Left to right: Christine Gonzalez, Liam Kenny, Miriam Ni Chleirigh, Fanchea Gibson, Mary McNamara, Margaret McCann, Richard Dowling, Joanna Travers

The staff of the Mansion House during 2014 and into 2015 are:

- Fanchea Gibson, Administrative Officer
- Margaret McCann, Diary Secretary to the Lord Mayor
- Christine Gonzalez, Assistant Staff Officer
- Miriam Ní Chleirigh, Assistant Staff Officer
- Joanna Travers, Clerical Officer
- Richard Dowling, House Steward
- Liam Kenny, House Steward
- Mary McNamara, Cleaner
- Michelle Sallinger, Cleaner
- Jimmy Hogarty, Lord Mayor's Driver
- Noel Hogarty, Lord Mayor's Driver

In addition Ray Glynn and Frank Molloy assist the staff of the Mansion House as Reserve House Steward and Reserve Lord Mayor's Driver during times of leave. The Aide-de-Camps to the Lord Mayors during 2014 were:

- Joe Trimble
- Ray Murray
- Derek Fox

APPENDIX 3: ARCHITECTURAL DESCRIPTION OF THE MAIN PUBLIC RECEPTION ROOMS

Susan Roundtree

As a sequence of spaces the interiors of the Mansion House are of particular interest. The earliest accounts of the house clearly describe the design intent and detail of the interiors and allow an invaluable insight into the development of interior trends over time. We are fortunate in having an early description of the house from the original purchase agreement. The twentieth century Sibthorpe interior schemes are also reasonably well documented and the photographs that survive of the interiors from c.1910 are of great value in understanding the evolution of the present day interior.

Entrance Hall

This is a square room with painted raised-and-fielded panelling that dates from 1710. The authenticity of the panelling is confirmed by its detailing. A jib door in the panelling behind the mahogany bookcase on the right hand side connects to a cupboard in the Lord Mayor's study. The door cases to the two front rooms are original but the doors have been altered as has the panelling overhead. The doors to the Staircase Hall and Dining Room lobby have 1760s architraves and late nineteenth century over doors. The chimney piece is of black polished Kilkenny marble with fossilised shells and dates from about 1765. The fireplace opening is flanked by engaged Doric columns which support an entablature with a plain frieze and moulded cornice. The centre of the frieze has a plain plaque.

The front door dates from the 1760s and has a contemporary architrave. It is boarded in a diamond pattern and retains its massive iron L-shaped hinges and an early security chain. The door also has a Georgian mahogany box lock with brass mounts. The floor of the hall is of Portland stone with some York stone flags used for later repairs. The ceiling

The Mansion House Entrance Hall
(Alastair Smeaton)

Georgian mahogany lock on
Mansion House front door
(Conor McCabe)

is decorated with a panelled raised paper which is noted in works described as taking
place in the house in 1900.

Lady Mayoress Parlour

This parlour was originally called the 'Walnut Parlour', later the 'Gilt Room' and more
recently the 'Blue Room'. The square proportions of the parlour are original to the
house constructed by Joshua Dawson but the interior decoration dates from the early
nineteenth century. The room has a corner chimney breast with a chimney piece of
white marble, inlaid with yellow Siena marble on the side jambs and frieze. The room
is finished with a coved decorative plaster cornice and centre piece attributed to the
Dublin stuccodore Charles Thorp (Lord Mayor of Dublin 1800-01). Thorp is also credited
with the decorative plasterwork in the coffee room at The Royal Exchange (now City
Hall Council Chamber), The Blue Coat School, and also several houses in North Great

(Left) Overview of the Lady Mayoress Parlour
(Conor McCabe)

(Right) Lady Mayoress Parlour:
View of the Sibthorpe decorative
scheme, c.1900
(Irish Architectural Archive)

George's Street and Hume Street. He also developed a number of houses on Mountjoy Square. The wide floorboards in the room are of pitch pine and are the only early boards to survive in the house on this floor. The windows and their joinery date from the mid nineteenth century. One of the windows on the north side has been changed to a pair of French doors which allow for the room to be opened to the garden on formal occasions.

Drawing Room

The room was originally called the 'Danzick Oak Parlour' but became known as the 'Drawing Room' in about 1821. The present form of the room dates from alterations of 1763. The windows are of similar date with raised-and-fielded shutters although now with Victorian sashes. The double doors to the Oak Room were first inserted in 1864 by city architect, Hugh Byrne, but were subsequently widened to the current arrangement, probably when the single door adjacent to this opening was closed up in the 1930s.

The room was re-styled in about 1900 by the firm of Sibthorpe, interior designers and decorators under the direction of the City Architect, Charles McCarthy. The chandeliers, lamps, fireplace brasses, fan, decorative ceiling plasterwork and over mantle mirror date from the Sibthorpe work. The white marble chimney piece is mid-nineteenth century.

Main Staircase Hall

The main staircase remains practically unaltered from its 1710 origin. The walls are panelled with raised-and-fielded panels. The staircase is wide and in two flights of dog-leg design without a continuous handrail. The treads are open with hand carved bracket ends. The balusters are hand carved tapered barley twist columns with three columns dovetailed into each tread board. The handrail and balusters have been identified as being made from Yew wood (Taxus Baccata), which is an unusual timber for joinery work, although not for furniture.

The stained glass window located on the half landing was inserted in anticipation of Home Rule in 1900 and made by the Dublin firm of Joshua Clarke and Sons. It features the

(Left) The balusters on the Main Staircase date from c. 1710.
(Joanna Travers)

(Right) Stained glass window by Joshua Clarke & Sons, 1900
(Alastair Smeaton)

official Lord Mayor's coat-of-arms, surrounded in turn by the coat-of-arms of the four provinces of Ireland. The panels show the names of notable Irishmen - writer Oliver Goldsmith, politicians Edmund Burke and Daniel O'Connell, the newspaper editor Sir John Gray, the actor Spranger Barry and the sculptor John Henry Foley. Joshua Clarke was the father of Harry Clarke who became a world famous stained glass artist.

The Oak Room

This room was built as part of the purchase agreement with Joshua Dawson in 1715. He undertook 'to make a large room, according to the plan annexed, and to wainscot and finish it completely, and paint it, and also to make a room under it of the same bigness for servants or officers'. It was to be thirty three feet ten inches long and twenty five feet wide. Before he could proceed with his plans, the location was changed to the north east end of the house and the design enlarged, the Corporation paying the extra expense this entailed.

The beauty of the room was widely appreciated. When William Tighe (MP for Wicklow) added a south wing to his house at Rossanagh, Co. Wicklow, in 1784, his new salon was compared with the Oak Room in the Mansion House which was noted as being one of the best panelled rooms in Ireland. Described as the 'Ball Room' by Wright in 1825, he notes that it was lined with wainscoting of Irish oak, containing two chimney pieces and linked directly to the Round Room.

Today the room measures twenty five feet by forty six feet and seven inches. While still panelled with oak it was substantially altered as a result of the building of the lobby and passageway between the Round Room and the Supper Room. This alteration removed its direct connection with the Round Room and four windows on the north side of the room which are described in the Georgian Society Records of 1912. The roof of the Oak Room was reconstructed in 1934 and the room is now top lit by means of three large lantern roof lights. Later the same year the entire reconstruction of the room was deemed necessary. There is no sign today of the fireplaces described by Wright or in the

Georgian Society Records in 1912. One of these fireplaces had a special bracket nearby for supporting the civic sword and maces. Some wall panelling of superior quality does survive in the room but most of the panelling is of twentieth century date. At basement level it is possible to get a sense of the original form of the room which in earlier times served as a kitchen.

Panoramic view of the Oak Room
(Conor McCabe)

The two chandeliers in the room are Waterford Crystal and were purchased in 1977 with funds raised from the sale of redundant furniture stored in the basement. The chandeliers have recently been fitted with LED lamps as part of an energy efficiency retrofit project carried out at the Mansion House in 2010.

One of two Waterford Crystal chandeliers in the Oak Room
(Conor McCabe)

The Dining Room

This room was described as the 'Large Eating Room' in 1715 and as the 'Sheriffs' Room' in 1821. The interior of the room dates in part from the 1760s and retains its mid-Georgian style in its joinery and decoration. The shouldered door and window architraves are typically 1760s. The doors themselves are earlier and are very slim. The black marble chimneypiece, in Egyptian style, is very interesting and dates from around 1830. The opening is flanked by caryatid terms with folded arms supporting a panelled frieze with a central plaque depicting a sphinx. The wide shelf has a reeded base. The pier mirror over the mantelpiece is late Georgian and matches the mirror in the entrance hall. The mahogany extending dining table is Victorian. The chairs and carvers are Edwardian.

The double doors to the east end of the room were inserted in 1864 connecting the room initially to a Supper Room which later became a Billiards Room. The staff administrative offices now occupy this part of the building. Prior to this date the east end of the room had a bow window looking to the rear garden which was inserted in 1763.

Lord Mayor's Office

This room was described as the 'Exchequer' in 1821. It has been used as the Lord Mayor's Office since the early years of the twentieth century. The room originally connected to the Dining Room with a door that matched the connecting door that still exists between the Lady Mayoress's Parlour and the Drawing Room. The office was originally panelled in Irish oak which was removed in the 1970s. The window casings, shutters and seats in oak survive. The shutters have raised-and-fielded panels and surviving original hinges and fittings. The timber cornice also survives in this room. The wooden chimney piece is modern and dates from c.1920.

(Right) The Dining Room today
(Dublin City Architect's Section)

(Left) The Dining Room
View of the Sibthorpe decorative
scheme, c.1900
(Irish Architectural Archive)

APPENDIX 4: CATALOGUE OF FURNITURE IN THE MANSION HOUSE

Patricia Wrafter

Entrance Hall

1. *An Edwardian, Georgian style cast iron and brass serpentine front dog grate decorated urn with shaped finials and pierced apron and a pair of attendant fire dogs with a Victorian brass and cast iron fire grate, the railed front above a fret pierced frieze, flanked by a stepped square section uprights with urn finials and splayed legs, late 19th century.*
   c. 1880.
   31" long x 12"deep x 27" wide (780 mm x 300mm x 680mm)
   Provenance: Original to Mansion House
   Description: Inspiration for this design may come from the 1765 edition of 'The smith's right hand'. Plates 13: two very neat designs for stove grates with Chinese frets ....made by Messers W and J Weldon, London, 1765. There is no evidence to date of an Irish edition of this pattern book.

2. *A set of three timber painted tipstaffs with brass mounts*
   Date unknown.
   61 ½" long (1981mm)
   Description: Three painted timber tipstaffs with brass mounts which were carried by officials of the Lord Mayor's Court – the Lord Mayor was Chief Magistrate of the city.

3. *A George III mahogany breakfront composed bookcase with moulded cornice above four astragal glazed doors on a deep cupboard base, fitted one long centre drawer and twin panel door cupboard with oval insets flanked with cupboards with false drawers fascia, bearing a brass plaque inscribed 'Bookcase formerly in the Irish House of Lords, presented to the Irish Home Rule League by Mitchell Henry Esq., MP'.*
   c. 1760.
   90" high x 111" wide (2286mm x 2819mm).
   Provenance: Original to House of Lords and then the Mansion House.

4. *A set of four Regency carved mahogany hall chairs with curved panel backs, the cartouches painted with the arms of the city of Dublin, having panel seats and raised on turned and reeded tapering legs.*
   c. 1820–25
   Provenance: Original to Mansion House possibly to coincide with the visit of George IV to the Mansion House in 1821.Possibly by Williams and Gibton, Dublin.
   Note: Evidence of substantial repairs on chairs therefore difficult to accurately identify them.

5. *A late Victorian stained beech stick barometer inscribed 'Yeates and Sons Dublin'.*
   c. 1880.
   40" high x 8" wide (1016mm x 200mm)
   Provenance: Original to Mansion House

6. *An Irish Georgian mahogany rectangular side table, the top raised above a chinoiserie blind fret frieze depicting a central lotus pattern and with compressed lozenges with a gothic quatrefoil and double loop patterns, gothic on four square legs.*
   75" x19.5" (1900mm x 483mm wide)
   c. 1760.
   Provenance: Original to Mansion House

7. *A Regency style 19th century giltwood rectangular pier mirror, the moulded cornice above a frieze decorated with applied rosettes, the triple compartmented mirror with beaded astragal bars, flanked by pairs of cluster columns with acanthus leaf capitals. May be part of the original Sibthorpe decorative scheme located in the Lady Mayoress' Parlour. A pair to one in the Dining Room.*
   c. 1880.
   86" x 58" (26213mm x 17678mm)

8. *A George III Mahogany longcase clock with swan neck pediment, having applied rosettes, and blind fret frieze, the brass dial inscribed "George Walker Dublin"[1] , flanked by fluted pillars, above a shaped panel door on a platform base.*
   c. 1760.
   90" high x 20" wide x 10" deep (2300mm high x 500mm wide x 260mm deep)
   Provenance: 'Sponsored for The Mansion House by The Harvard Graduates Association in Ireland for Dublin Millennium Year 1988'.

1. Fireplace in Entrance Hall surmounted by portrait of Daniel O'Connell surrounded by tipstaffs (Joanna Travers)

2. Brass head of tipstaff in Entrance Hall (Conor McCabe)

3. Breakfront bookcase in Entrance Hall (Conor McCabe)

4. One of four hall chairs in Entrance Hall (Joanna Travers)

5. Barometer in Entrance Hall (Joanna Travers)

6 & 7. Rectangular side table in Entrance Hall with hall chairs in place surmounted by giltwood rectangular pier mirror (Joanna Travers)

8. Longcase clock in Entrance Hall (Joanna Travers)

9. *A Victorian cast iron rectangular umbrella and stick stand with the following numbers under the frame.*
154   9 ¾
Trays at bottom also have numbers:
2 ½   2 ¾
c. 1860.
20" x 11" (508mm x 279mm)
Provenance: Original to the Mansion House.

Lady Mayoress' Parlour[2]

10. *An Inlaid Rosewood circular dining table, the crossbanded top with brass stringing and quatrefoil motifs, raised on a square waisted centrepillar and quadruped platform base with paw feet*
c. 1825–1835.
56 ½" in diameter (1435mm)
Provenance: Original to Mansion House. The large circular table is a fine example of Irish craftsmanship [3] and was made between 1825 and 1835 and was *possibly* bought for the Mansion House for the visit of George 1V in 1821.

11. *A 19th century French Louis Seize style giltwood five piece salon suite comprising a two seater settee, a pair of armchairs and a pair of side chairs, the panel backs a carved and curved rail and framed by fluted columns, upholstered and covered in blue silk damask, and raised on turned fluted tapered legs.*
c. Second half of 19th century when there was a revival of Louis Seize style
Provenance: Original to Mansion House.

12-13. *A pair of George 1V inlaid mahogany shaped rectangular folding top card tables, decorated boxwood stringing, rosewood banding and raised on turned tapering legs.*
C. 1820–1840
Provenance: Original to Mansion House. They were *possibly* bought for the Mansion House for the visit of George 1V in 1821, but are not grand.

14. *A Regency giltwood overmantle mirror, the moulded cornice with applied ball decoration above a frieze depicting a chariot pulled by lions in classical procession in bas relief, the central section inset with Victorian alterations with hand tinted print depicting the three graces with Victorian machine bevelled inset, flanked by rectangular regency hand bevelled side mirror panels and cluster column supports.*
c. 1820–1840
55" width (1400mm)
Provenance: Original to Mansion House. It was *possibly* bought for the Mansion House for the visit of George 1V in 1821.

15-16. *A pair of Edwardian mahogany framed armchairs with incised ladder backs, padded seats and raised on square tapering legs and spade feet and doweled joints.*
c. 1901–1910.
Provenance: Probably part of the Sibthorpe scheme for the Mansion House c.1900.

17. *An Edwardian inlaid walnut and fruitwood octagonal top centre table raised on turned column supports and undertier.*
22.5" in diameter (506mm)
Provenance: The Mansion House

9. Umbrella Stand in Mansion House Entrance Hall (Joanna Travers)

10. Rosewood table from Lady Mayoress' Parlour (Joanna Travers)

11. Two-seater settee in Louis Seize style from suite in Lady Mayoress' Parlour (Joanna Travers)

Chair in Louis Seize style with arms from Lady Mayoress' Parlour (Joanna Travers)

12-13. One of two inlaid mahogany card tables, open from Lady Mayoress' Parlour (Joanna Travers)

14. Overmantle mirror from Lady Mayoress' Parlour (Joanna Travers)

15-16. Ladderback chair from the Lady Mayoress' Parlour (Joanna Travers)

17. Edwardian inlay octagonal table from Lady Mayoress' Parlour (Joanna Travers)

18. *A modern Irish octagonal wool carpet, the centre circular medallion within a beige field decorated with ribbon and flower trailing sprays in pale blue, yellow and rose. Pattern echoes stucco design in ceiling.*
183" in diameter. (4650mm)
Provenance: Hand-made in Connemara by J.D. McMurray of Moyard, Co. Galway to mark the Dublin Millennium celebrations in 1988.

19. *An Art Nouveau tubular brass framed shaped oval fire screen with segmented stained glass panel*
33.5" high, 27" wide. (805mm x 609mm)
Provenance: Part of the Sibthorpe decoration scheme c. 1900.

Drawing Room [4]

20. *A Victorian Louis Quatorze ebony and Boulle shaped bureau plat, with cast brass egg, dart and swag rim, above a single frieze drawer and raised on cabriole legs with applied brass figural mounts.*
c. 1880.
35" x 59" (889mm x 1499mm)

21. *Another Similar*
c. 1880.
37" x 64" (904mm x 1,600mm)
Provenance: Original to Mansion House
One table was already in Mansion House and then another was bought by Lord Mayor Alfie Byrne and his wife, to match from James Adam Auctioneers, at a later date.

22. *A Victorian Rococo carved giltwood overmantle mirror on an ebonised plinth with 'C' scrolls and pierced decoration raised on an ebonised plinth (regilded).*
c. 1870
96" x 83" (2,438mm x 2,413mm)
Provenance: Original to Mansion House. Part of Sibthorpe decorative scheme for the Drawing Room.

23. *A Victorian French style brass retractable fan shaped spark guard*
c. 1870
96" x 83" high (2438mm x 2108mm)
Provenance: Original to Mansion House. Part of Sibthorpe decorative scheme for the drawing room.

24. *A modern "Petrof" model three ebony cased baby grand piano with cover and piano stool.*
c. Late 20th century.
Provenance: The Mansion House. On long-term loan from College of Music

25. *A Pair of Victorian metal figural lamps of male and female figures below twin light branches.*
25" high (635mm high).
Provenance: Original to Mansion House. Part of Sibthorpe decorative scheme for the Drawing Room.

26. *A 19th Century ebonised timber cased bracket clock with brass mounts the movement with Westminster chimes by M. Anderson Dublin, raised on cast brass bracket feet.*
c. 1890
28" high (711mm)
Provenance: Original to Mansion House. Part of Sibthorpe decorative scheme for the Drawing Room.

18. Hand-made octagonal carpet from Lady Mayoress' Parlour
(Joanna Travers)

22. Overmantle mirror in Drawing Room with clock and light fittings
(Joanna Travers)

25. Figure as part of lamp in Drawing Room
(Conor McCabe)

19. Oval firescreen from the Lady Mayoress' Parlour
(Joanna Travers)

23. Spark guard in Drawing Room
(Joanna Travers)

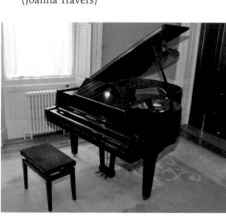

24. Petrof grand piano in Drawing Room
(Joanna Travers)

20. Boulle table in Drawing Room
(Joanna Travers)

26. Bracket clock from Mansion House
(Conor McCabe)

27. *A George IV inlaid mahogany shaped rectangular folding top card table, decorated boxwood stringing, rosewood banding and raised on turned tapering legs.*
c. 1820–1840
Provenance: Original to Mansion House. It was *possibly* bought for the Mansion House for the visit of George IV in 1821, but is not grand.

28. *Late 18th century English or Irish Chippendale window bench[5] or window seat, the square legs with H-stretcher and outswept upholstered arms. The entire has been cut down lengthways, thus the unusual shape. Bench is covered in a nautical blue floral damask.*
c. 1770
52" x 24" (700mm x 600mm high).
Provenance: Original to Mansion House.

Dining Room

29. *A Regency style century giltwood rectangular pier mirror, the moulded cornice above a frieze decorated with applied rosettes, the triple compartmented mirror with beaded astragal bars, flanked by pairs of cluster columns with acanthus leaf capitals. A pair to one in the Entrance Hall.*
c. 1880.
86"x 58" (2159mm x 1473mm)
Provenance: Original to Mansion House. May be part of Sibthorpe scheme, originally located in the Lord Mayor's Office.

30. *A Victorian Mahogany telescopic extending dining table with moulded rim raised on heavy carved baluster legs with fluted legs. (7 leaves)*
c. 1860
229" x 60 ½" (5817mm x 1830mm)
Provenance: Original to the Mansion House.

31. *A set of 18 Edwardian Mahogany rail back chairs on turned legs.*
c. 1900.
Provenance: Original to Mansion House. May be part of Sibthorpe scheme.

32-3. *A pair of Edwardian stained oak arm chairs with padded inset. Raised on turned tapering legs.*
c. 1900.
Provenance: Original to Mansion House.

34. *A large 19th Century gilt console table with a Sienna marble top with panels on pink marble banded in blue. The table with an apron carved with fruit swags and a cartouche on cabriole legs.*
c. 1870.
84" x 23" (2134mm x 584mm)
Provenance: Original to Mansion House.

35. *Two end panel sections of a set of four sections of a Victorian extending dining table (The other two sections are stored elsewhere.)*
c. 1860.
206" x 80" (5232mm x 2032mm)
Provenance: Original to Mansion House.

36-7. *An important pair of Rosewood and Parcel Gilt library armchairs, the entire with fine quality Acanthus leaf and scroll carving. The front legs carved and fluted. The rear legs swept back and ending in a French turned up toe. Probably by Williams and Gibton of Dublin.*
c. 1820.
Provenance: Original to the Mansion House. They were possibly obtained for the visit of George IV.

38-9. *A pair of 20th Century Mahogany serpentine side tables, in the Adam style. The centre table with carved urn and swags, flanked by a fluted frieze. The tapering fluted legs surmounted by carved patterae. Stamped by James Hicks.*
c. Early 20th century
84" x 23" (2134mm x 584mm)
Provenance: James Hicks dining room side tables were given to Dublin Corporation to mark the Dublin Millennium by the Friends of the National Collections of Ireland. The tables have been installed in the Dining Room in the Mansion House where the organisation had their annual general meeting.

40. *A Victorian inlaid black marble mantle clock.*
13 ½" wide x 17" high (340mm x 432mm)
Provenance: Original to Mansion House and part of Sibthorpe decorative scheme for the Drawing Room.

41. *A George III inlaid Mahogany longcase clock with broken pediment above a painted white dial. The panel door flanked by fluted pilasters on a platform base and bracket feet.*
c. Latter part of 18th century.
87" high (2210mm)
Provenance: As part of 1987 Jefferson Smurfit donation to Mansion House for Dining Room including longcase clock.

27. Card table from Drawing Room
(Conor McCabe)

30. Dining Room with Edwardian dining chairs
and two large carvers (Joanna Travers)

38-39. One of two James Hicks side tables in
Dining Room (Joanna Travers)

28. Chippendale window bench, c. 1770
(Joanna Travers)

34. Console table in the Dining Room
(Conor McCabe)

40. Victorian marble mantle clock from the
Dining Room
(Joanna Travers)

29. Overmantle mirror in Dining Room
(Conor McCabe)

35. One of the two end-panel table sections
from a Victorian Dining Table from the
Dining Room (Joanna Travers)

36-37. Tableau composed of two library
armchairs, mahogany cutlery chest
and silverware from the Dining Room
(Conor McCabe)

41. George III inlaid mahogany longcase clock
from the Dining Room
(Joanna Travers)

42. *A set of 8 Edwardian Mahogany salon chairs (of which two are elbow chairs) on turned legs. The cresting rail carved with official arms of Lord Mayor of Dublin, including the Cap of Maintenance.*
    c. 1900.
    Provenance: Original to Mansion House. May be part of Sibthorpe decorative scheme.

43. *A Victorian oak framed brass dinner gong and beater.*
    c. 1880.
    27.5" wide and 47" high
    (696mm x 1194mm)
    Provenance: Original to Mansion House.

44. *A mahogany rectangular cutlery chest and other flatware store with fitted interior, triple carved panel front.*
    Provenance: Original to Mansion House. May be part of Sibthorpe decorative scheme.

Oak Room

45. *A pair of twentieth century Waterford cut and polished glass twenty-five light chandeliers with three tiers of scroll branches decorated with icicle pendants designed 'in the Georgian manner.'*
    Latter part of the 20th century.
    Provenance: Mansion House.

46. Series of coats of arms for each Lord Mayor of Dublin since Daniel O'Connell displayed as wooed plaques affixed to Oak Room walls.

Staircase Hall

47. *An 18th Century half moon folding card table on square tapering legs.*
    c. 1790.
    37" x 18"
    (940mm x 457mm x 760mm)
    Provenance: Original to Mansion House. It may be English or Irish[6].

Other Items Of Furniture

48. *A Harlequin set of twenty Louis Quinze style carved giltwood framed upholstered salon chairs, decorated shells, leaf scrolls and 'C' scroll borders, covered in pale blue water silk and with ormolu mounts raised on cabriole legs.' And decorated at seat level with shell motifs. Cresting rail with ornate brass carrying handles.*
    c. 1880.
    Provenance: The chairs were purchased at Cabinteely House sale and presented to Mansion House by Jefferson Smurfit plc .to mark the Dublin Millennium in 1988.

Chimney Pieces

49. *Entrance Hall, chimney piece in black Kilkenny limestone with fossils*
    c. 1760.
    Provenance: The Mansion House. 'This black Kilkenny marble chimney piece dates from c.1765.The ope is flanked by engaged Doric Columns which supports the entablature with a plain frieze and moulded cornice. The centre of the frieze is ornamented with a plain plaque. This chimney piece is similar to that in the dining room of Newbridge House, but lacks the broken pediment.' Confirmed by the Knight of Glin in 2009. Note the fine detail of fossilised shells in the limestone.

42. Salon chair bearing the Lord Mayor's Crest from the Dining Room (Joanna Travers)

44. Mahogany cutlery chest from the Dining Room (Joanna Travers)

45. Waterford Crystal Chandelier from the Oak Room (Conor McCabe)

48. One of a Harlequin set of twenty Louis Quinze chairs for the Dining Room (Joanna Travers)

49. Chimney piece in front hall (Joanna Travers)

43. Victorian oak framed brass dinner gong and beater from the Dining Room (Joanna Travers)

46. Arms of Sir George Moyers Lord Mayor of Dublin 1881 from the Oak Room (Conor McCabe)

50. *Lady Mayoress' Parlour, chimney piece in white marble with sienna marble insets*
    18th century with 19th and 20th century additions.
    Provenance: Indicated in the Sibthorpe scheme.

51. *Drawing Room, chimney piece in white marble*
    c. 1840

52. *Dining Room, chimney piece in black limestone in Regency style*
    c. 1820–30.
    Provenance: Original to the Mansion House.

Significant Light Fixtures
Entrance Hall

53. *A 19th Century Louis Philippe cast brass electrolier, the spiral turned columns with opening acanthus flower collar supporting a circular body and four scroll branches with engraved glass bulbous shades.*
    c. 1880.
    Provenance: Original to Mansion House. Part of the Sibthorpe scheme decoration of circa 1900. Possibly supplied by Sibthorpe.

Drawing Room

54. *A pair of Victorian style brass ten light electroliers with cast foliate scroll branches and etched glass shades.*
    c. 1900
    Provenance: Original to Mansion House. Part of the Sibthorpe scheme decoration of circa 1900.

Drawing Room

55. *A pair of bronze overhanging mantle double overhanging lights and acid etched/frosted bell profile frosted glass shades.*
    c. 1900.
    Provenance: Original to Mansion House. Part of the Sibthorpe scheme decoration of circa 1900.Possibly supplied by Sibthorpe.

Staircase Hall and lobby

56. *A 20th Century brass bevelled hexagonal glass hall lantern with finials and turned feet. Electric lighting.*
    c. Latter part of 20th century.
    Provenance: Original to Mansion House. Part of the Sibthorpe scheme decoration of circa 1900. Possibly supplied by Sibthorpe.

Occasional Silverware

57. *Silver spade belonging to Alfie Byrne Lord Mayor of Dublin 1930–1939 and 1954–55. By Thomas Weir of Dublin.*
    The silver blade, and shaft socket, are richly engraved with Celtic patterns, as are also the silver ferrules at the terminations of the shaft and handle. The blade is inscribed 'Presented to the Right Honourable the Lord Mayor, Alderman Alfred Byrne, Senator, On the occasion of cutting the first sod for the construction of additional slow sand filters at Dublin Corporation Waterworks, Roundwood, Co. Wicklow. 15th Sept. 1931. Grainger Bros., Contractors'. The lettering, appropriately, is of the old Irish type. This beautiful example of Irish silver-work was executed by Thomas Weir, whose hallmark is inscribed on the rear of the blade. The shaft is 26 inches long, and the handle (curved) is 31.5 31.5inches, and both are of mahogany.

50. Chimney piece in Lady Mayoress' Parlour
(Alastair Smeaton)

52. Chimney piece in the Dining Room
(Joanna Travers)

56. Lantern from Staircase Hall
(Joanna Travers)

53. Electrolier from Entrance Hall
(Joanna Travers)

51. Chimney piece in Drawing Room
(Joanna Travers)

54. One of a pair of electroliers from
Drawing Room
(Joanna Travers)

57. Silver spade presented to Lord Mayor
Alfie Byrne.

58. *Joshua Dawson Cup. Made in Dublin 1712-13 by Thomas Bolton. Inscribed on base 'Ex Dono Joshua Dawson 1714' indicating that it was a gift from him to an unknown recipient. The contemporary crest engraving is biblical in content and may indicate a connection to St. Ann's Church. Purchased by Dublin City Council 2015 to mark the tercentenary of the Mansion House.*

6" high, 9" wide including handles

58. Joshua Dawson Cup: side engraved with lamb
(J.W. Weldon)

Joshua Dawson Cup:
Base engraved 'Ex Dono Iosua Dawson Anno 1714'
(J.W. Weldon)

Joshua Dawson Cup: Detail of engraved lamb
(J.W. Weldon)

APPENDIX 5: CATALOGUE OF PORTRAITS IN THE MANSION HOUSE

Mary Clark

Entrance Hall
O'CONNELL, Daniel
John Gubbins
Three quarter length, standing by a table, with silver drinking cup
Oil on canvas
Size: 60" x 48" (1524 x 1219 mm)

Staircase Hall
GEORGE IV
Sir Thomas Lawrence, 1821
Full length, standing in Garter robes
Oil on canvas
Size: 120" x 81" (3048 x 2053 mm)

Oak Room
FOSTER, John
Last Speaker of the Irish House
of Commons
Hugh Douglas Hamilton, 1799
Full length, standing wearing robes of office
Oil on canvas
Size: 97" x 59" (2463 x 1498 mm)

Oak Room

MANDERS, Richard (*died* **1823)**

Lord Mayor of Dublin, 1801–1802

Robert Francis West, 1802

Full length, standing wearing mayoral robes and chain, holding wand of office, with city sword and mace

Oil on canvas

Size: 93" x 61" (2362 x 1549 mm)

Dining Room

ABBOTT, Thomas

Lord Mayor of Dublin, 1825-26

Nicholas A. Crowley

Half-length, standing wearing mayoral robes and chain, holding wand of office

Oil on canvas

Size: 45" x 35" (1142 x 889 mm)

Dining Room (continued)

STAUNTON, Michael (1788–1870)

Lord Mayor of Dublin, 1847

Artist unknown

Half length, wearing a black jacket and cravat

Oil on canvas

Size: 30" x 25" (761 x 635 mm)

Oak Room

PARNELL, Charles Stewart

Leader of the Home Rule Party

Sir Thomas Alfred Jones PRHA, 1892

[signed and dated]

Three quarter length, standing in a nocturnal landscape, with ruined church

Oil on canvas

Size: 50" x 40" (1270 x 1016 mm)

Dining Room

PEARSON, Sir Nathaniel

Lord Mayor of Dublin, 1730-31

Artist unknown

Three quarter length, wearing mayoral robes and chain, holding wand of office, with city sword and mace

Oil on canvas

Size: 50" x 40" (1270 x 1016 mm)

Dining Room

STAUNTON, Mrs. Michael (*nee* **Anne Overend)**

Lady Mayoress of Dublin, 1847

Artist unknown

Half length, wearing a black dress with lace sleeves

Oil on canvas

Size: 30" x 25" (761 x 635 mm)

Drawing Room

**TOWNSHEND, George 4th Viscount
and 1st Marquis**

Lord Lieutenant of Ireland, 1767-72

Thomas Hickey, 1769 *[signed and dated]*

*Full length, standing wearing robes of office,
holding the act for limiting the duration
of Parliament*

Oil on canvas

Size: 90" x 58" (2286 x 1473 mm)

Dining Room

**BUCKINGHAM, George Villiers,
1st duke of**

After Daniel Mytens

*Full length portrait, standing wearing
a lace ruff, against a coastal landscape
with horsemen and sailing ships*

Oil on canvas

Size: 92" x 55" (2336 x 1397 mm)

Dining Room

**RICHMOND and LENNOX,
Charles Lennox, 4th Duke of**

Lord Lieutenant of Ireland, 1807-13

William Cuming, 1813

Full length, standing wearing Garter robes

Oil on canvas

Size: 99" x 64" (2514 x 1626 mm)

Dining Room

**BUCKINGHAM, George Nugent-Temple-
Grenville, 1st Marquis of**

Lord Lieutenant of Ireland, 1782-83
and 1787-89

Solomon Williams, 1789

frame by John Smith Cranfield, 1789

*Full length portrait, standing wearing
ceremonial robes*

Oil on canvas

Size: 94" x 62" (2387 x 1575 mm)

Drawing Room

**NORTHUMBERLAND, Hugh Smithson,
2nd Earl and 1st Duke of**

Lord Lieutenant of Ireland, 1763-65

Sir Joshua Reynolds, 1765

Full length, standing wearing robes of office

Oil on canvas

Size: 90" x 58" (2286 x 1473 mm)

Drawing Room

WESTMORLAND, John Fane 10th Earl of

Lord Lieutenant of Ireland, 1790-95

George Romney, 1795

*Full length, standing wearing robes
of office*

Oil on canvas

Size: 96" x 60" (2439 x 1524 mm)

APPENDIX 6: TRANSCRIPT OF THE ORIGINAL DEED TO THE MANSION HOUSE

Christian Keegan

This indenture made the Eighteenth day of May in the Yeare of Our Lord one thousand seven hundred and fifteen, and in the first Year of the Reigne of our Sovereigne Lord George By the Grace of God of Great Brittain, France and Ireland King Defender of the Faith &c. Between Joshua Dawson of the City of Dublin Esqre of the one part, and the Right Honourable Sir James Barlow Knight Lord Mayor of the said City of Dublin, Peter Verdoen, and William Aldrich Esqres Sheriffes of the said City, and the Comons and Citizens of the said City of Dublin of the other part. Whereas Henry Temple of East Shaen in the County of Surrey in the Kingdom of England Esqre by his deed indented and duely executed under his hand and Seale bearing date the one and twentyth day of March in the year of Our Lord God one thousand seven hundred and five, made between the said Henry Temple of the one part, and the said Joshua Dawson of the other part, for the considerations therein mentioned, did grant Bargaine, sell, alien, remise, release and confirm onto the said Joshua Dawson his Heires and Assignes for ever, all that and those houses, outhouses, Gardens, Parke or Parcell of land bounded on the West by Grafton Street, on the North by the highway leading to St. Patricks Well, on the East by the land belonging to Robert Molesworth Esqre and on the South by Severall Gardens belonging to Mr. Ram, and others, part of the Lotts of St. Stephens Green, containing eight acres, two Roods and thirty four Pearches or thereabouts, be the same more or lesse, Subject to the Yearly Chief Rent of fifty pounds sterling and Six pence for every pound thereof as Receivers fees, as by the said Deed among Severall Covenants and clauses therein contained (Relation being thereunto had) may more fully appeare, on part of which said Granted and Released Premises, the said Joshua Dawson hath built a large dwelling house and other conveniences thereunto belonging.

And whereas in and by an Indented Deed bearing date the second day of September in the Yeare one thousand Six hundred Sixty and four, made and mentioned to be made between William Smith Esqre then Mayor of the said city of Dublin, Thomas Kirkham, and William Brooks Sheriffes of the said city, and the Comons and Citizens thereof of the one part, and Hugh Price of the said City Merchant of the other part, all that one part or Plott of Ground Scituate, lying, and being on the North Side of St. Stephens Green Dublin, being the twenty Sixth Lott of the said North Side, containing in Front or Square of the said Green sixty feet, and the like number of Sixty feet on the extream part backward, and on the West end thereof in length two hundred twenty four feet, and on the East end in length two hundred and forty four feet, was granted and conveyed by the said Mayor, Sheriffes, Comons and Citizens to the said Hugh Price and his Heires at and under a Yearly Rent of Nineteen Shillings and six pence.

And Whereas the said Part or Plott of Ground so granted and conveyed to the said Hugh Price is since then come by mesne, conveyances and assignments to the said Joshua Dawson and his Heires, on part where of the Kitchen, Stables and Coachhouses of the said Joshua Dawson belonging to and annexed to the said Dwelling house are built and erected, and the remaining part thereof is laid out and disposed of in the new street called Dawsons Street Where the said Lord Mayor, Sheriffes, Comons and Citizens being minded to buy a house for the constant Residence and Habitation of the Lord Mayor of the City of Dublin have come to an agreement with the said Joshua Dawson for the purchase of the said house, and of some Goods and Furniture mentioned in a Schedule hereunto annexed, and the Garden, Outhouses, and other Appurtenances there unto belonging, and also for that Parcell of Ground whereon the same now stands, according to the Dimensions, Mearing, and Boundary as followeth viz. on the West to Dawson Street in the Front four hundred twenty four feet and a half, on the North to other Ground of the said Joshua Dawsons, and is in depth on the North Side one hundred eighty two feet and three Inches, on the East with some Ground belonging to the said Robert Molesworth Esqre one hundred and seventy feet on the South with Ground belonging to Abell Ram Esqre eighty six feet, and with other Ground belonging to the said Abell Ram on the East two hundred fifty six feet three Inches, as by a Map of the said piece or parcell of Ground which is hereunto annexed may more fully and at large appear, he the said Joshua Dawson erecting and building, and causing to be forthwith erected and built, and added to the said house one other large Room of thirty three feet ten Inches long, twenty five feet wide, and fourteen feet high, to be well Wainscotted, Painted and completely finished, and to lease the said house, Outhouse and Garden in good repair, ready for the Reception of the next Lord Mayor.

Now This Indenture witnesseth that the said Joshua Dawson for and in consideration of the Sume of three thousand five hundred pounds sterling paid and agreed to be paid to him the said Joshua Dawson, by the said Lord Mayor, Sheriffes, Comons and Citizens of the said City of Dublin in manner following viz one thousand pounds part thereof in hand now paid the Receipt whereof the said Joshua Dawson doth hereby acknowledge, and thereof and of every part thereof doth herby acquit the said Lord Mayor, Sheriffes Comons and Citizens, and two thousand five hundred pounds more in three Yeares by three equal payments viz eight hundred thirty three pounds in six shillings and eight pence on the first of May one thousand Seven hundred and Sixteen, eight hundred thirty three pounds six shillings and eight pence on the first of May, one thousand Seven hundred and Seventeen, and the remaining eight hundred thirty three pounds six Shillings and eight pence on the first of May one thousand Seven hundred and eighteen, hath granted, bargained, sold, aliened, released and confirmed, and by these presents doth for him and his Heires fully clearly and absolutely grant, bargaine, sell, alien, remise, release and confirm unto the said Lord Mayor Sheriffes, Comons and Citizens of the said City of Dublin (in their actuall profession now being by virtue of a Bargain and Sale to them thereof made by the said Joshua Dawson for the Terme of one whole Yeare by Indenture bearing date, the day next before the date hereof, and by force of the Statute for transferring Uses into Profession) and to their Successors all that aforesaid piece or parcel of Ground continuing on the West to Dawsons Street in the Front four hundred twenty four feet, and a half, on the North side thereof one hundred eighty two feet, three Inches, on the East adjoyning to Mr. Molesworths Ground one hundred and Seventy feet, on the South eighty six feet, and on the East adjoining to Mr. Rams Ground two hundred fifty six feet three Inches, together with the house or Messuage thereon built, and the Goods and Furniture mentioned in the said Schedule annexed, and all Stables, Outhouses, Garden and other Appurtenances thereunto belonging in as large and ample manner as the said Joshua Dawson now holds and enjoys the same, and all the Estate, Right, Title, Interest, Use Possession, property, Claime, Challenge, and demand whatsoever of him the said Joshua Dawson and his Heires, of in or to the said hereby granted and Released Premises and every part thereof, by virtue of the said Recited Deeds or otherwise howsoever.

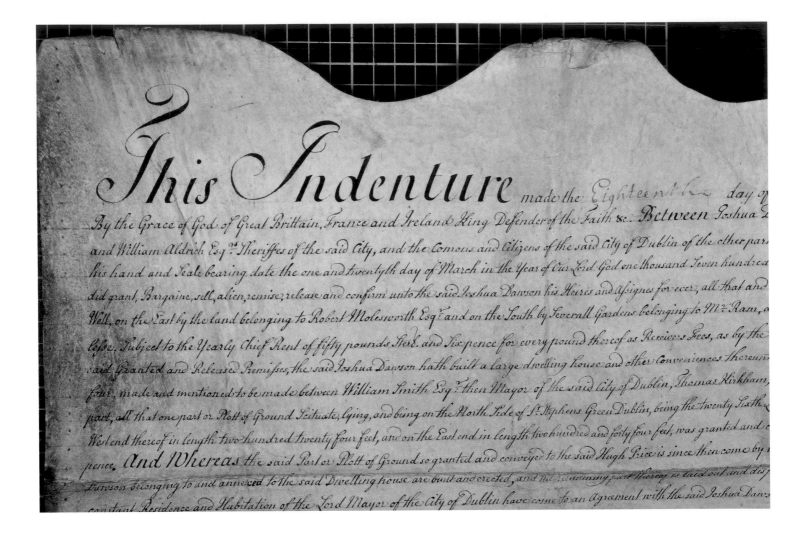

Detail of the indenture conveying the
Mansion House from Joshua Dawson to
the City of Dublin, 18 May 1714
(Alastair Smeaton)

To Have and to Hold the said hereby granted and Released Premises, with their
and every of their Appurtenances unto the said Lord Mayor, Sheriffes, Comons and
Citizens and their Successors for ever they the said Lord Mayor, Sheriffes Comons and
Citizens and their Successors, Yielding and Paying therefore and thereout Yearly and
every Yeare forever hereafter, the Rent of one Loaf of double refined Sugar of six pounds
weight at every Christmas Yearly, if the same shall be demanded, and the said Joshua
Dawson doth hereby bind and oblige himself his Heires, Executors, and Administrators
to erect and build and add to the said house one other large Room of thirty three feet
ten Inches long, twenty five feet wide, and fourteen feet high, and to wainscot, paint,
and finish the same compleatly, and to leave the house, Outhouses and Garden in good
repair ready for the reception of the next Lord Mayor, and to leave in the said house
all the Goods and Furniture mentioned in the said Schedule, and the said Lord Mayor,
Sheriffes, Comons and Citizens of the said City of Dublin do hereby bind them and
their Successors to pay unto the said Joshua Dawson his Executors Administrators or
Assignes the Sume of two thousand five hundred pounds which is to be paid by Gales
as aforesaid in manner following viz eight hundred Thirty Three pounds in Six Shillings
and eight pence on the first day of May one thousand seven hundred and sixteen the
like Sume of eight hundred thirty three pounds and six shillings and eight pence on the
first day of May one thousand seven hundred and seventeen, and the remaining eight

hundred thirty three pounds six shillings and eight pence on the first day of May one thousand seven hundred and eighteen,

And Whereas the said Henry Temple hath in and by the said recited Deed reserved from the said Joshua Dawson a yearly Rent of fifty pounds and Six pence per pound as Receivers fees payable out of part of the aforesaid Premises to which said Rent and Receivers fees part of the aforesaid Premises hereby granted and released are and may be lyable.

And Whereas also the said other part of the aforesaid Premises called the twenty sixth Lott on the said North Side of Stephens Green aforesaid is lyable to the payment of the said Yearly Rent of nineteen Shillings and six pence payable by the said fee forme deed so made to the Hugh Price.

Now to the intent and purpose that the said hereby granted and released Premises may from time to time for ever hereafter be cleared freed and discharged from the payment of the said Reserved Rents and fees, the said Joshua Dawson doth hereby give grant and confirm to the said Lord Mayor Sheriffes Comons and Citizens of the said City of Dublin, and their Successors, one annuity or Yearly Sume of fifty pounds twelve Shillings and six pence to be issuing and payable out of all that parcell of land bounded on the East by Dawson Street, on the South by Some of the City Lotts on St Stephens Green, on the West by Graftons Street, and on the North by Patricks Well Lane, which is part of the Ground so conveyed to him the said Joshua Dawson by him the said Henry Temple in and by the said Recited Deed.

To have and to hold the same to them the said Lord Mayor Sheriffes, Comons and Citizens and their Successors for ever to the Uses aforesaid, and the said Joshua Dawson doth for him his Heires and assignes give and grant full power and authority to them the said Lord Mayor, Sheriffes, Comons and Citizens of the said City of Dublin from time to time to enter and distraine for the said Annuity or Yearly Rent charge of fifty pounds twelve Shillings and six pence per pound Receivers fees according to Law in case this said Lord Mayor Sheriffs, Comons and Citizens of the said City of Dublin shall at any time be obliged to pay the said Reserved Rent of fifty pounds a Yeare or any part of thereof, and Receivers fees to which the Premises hereby granted are and may be lyable as aforesaid and to the end and intent that the said Lord Mayor, Sheriffes, Comons and Citizens of the said City of Dublin and their Successors for ever may be also freed, exonerated, acquitted and discharged of and from the said nineteen shillings and six pence per Annum payable and reserved in and by the said deed so made to the said Hugh Price the said Joshua Dawson doth by these presents further give and absolutely grant and confirm to the said Lord Mayor, Sheriffes, Comons and Citizens of the said City of Dublin and their successors for ever one annuity or Yearly charge of nineteen shillings and six pence to be issuing and payable yearly to the said Lord Mayor, Sheriffes, Comons and Citizens out of the aforesaid parcell of land so bounded on the East by Dawsons Street, on the South by some of the City's Lotts, on St. Stephens Green, on the West by Graftons Street, and on the North by Patricks Well Lane.

To have and to hold to them and their Successors to the only use and behoofe of them and their Successors for ever, and the said Joshua Dawson doth for him and his Heires give and grant full power, liberty and authority to them the said Lord Mayor Sheriffes Comons and Citizens, and their said Successors for ever, in case the said Rent charge of nineteen Shillings and Six pence shall be in arrears from time to time to enter into and distraine upon the Premises for the said Annuity or Yearly Rent charge of nineteen shillings and six pence, and to dispose of the Distress or Distresses that shall be so taken according to Law for satisfaction of the said Yearly Rent charge of nineteen shillings and six pence the arrears thereof, and the said Joshua Dawson for him his Heires Executors and Administrators doth hereby covenant promise grant and agree to and with the said Lord Mayor Sheriffes, Comons and Citizens and their Successors in manner following (that is to say) That for and notwithstanding any Act or thing by him the said Joshua Dawson or the said Henry Temple and Sir John Temple deceased Father of the said Henry Temple or the said Hugh Price or any of them, or any Person claiming by from or under them or any of them suffered to the contrary, the said herein before recited Deed is good and valid in the Law, and is, and stands in full force and virtue, and that he the said Joshua Dawson for and notwithstanding any such Act or thing by him the said Joshua Dawson the said Henry Temple and Sir John Temple deceased, or the said Hugh Price of any of them done or suffered to the contrary as aforesaid at or immediately before the ensealing and Delivery of these presents he shall himself good and lawfull and absolute authority [sell] and convey of Premises unto the said Lord Mayor, Sheriffes, Comons and Citizens, and their Successors in manner aforesaid and that all it shall and may be lawful to and for the said Lord Mayor, Sheriffes, Comons and Citizens and their Successors from time to time, and at all times for ever hereafter, Subject to Payment of the said Sugar, Loaf, Yearly, Peaceably and quietly to have, hold, use, occupy, possesse and enjoy all and singular the Premises hereby granted and released, or meant mentioned or intended to be hereby granted and released with their and every of their appurtenances without the Lett, Suite, Trouble, Eviction, Ejection, Deniall, hindrance or molestation of him the said Joshua Dawson his Heires, or Assignes, or the said Henry Temple his Heires or Assignes or the said Hugh Price his Heires or Assignes, or any other Person or Persons claiming to [....] by from or under them, either or any of them, or the said Sir John Temple deceased free and clear and freely and clearly acquitted exonerated and discharged or otherwise by the said Joshua Dawson and his Heires well and truely saved kept harmless and idemnifyed of and from all former and other Gifts, Grants, Bargaine, Sales, Assignments, Leases, Mortgages, Judgements, Executions, Extents, Recognizances, Rents,

(and particularly of and from the said Rent of fifty pounds sterling and Receivers fees reserved in and by the said recited Deed to the said Henry Temple, and also from the aforesaid Sume of nineteen Shillings and six pence a Yeare Reserved and made payable in and by the said fee farm deed so made to the said Hugh Price as aforesaid and all Suites and Distrainings on account thereof)

Rent charges, Uses [Thirds], Dowers, Wills, [Intailes], Troubles, Charges and Incumbrances whatsoever had, made, comitted, suffered, or done, or to be had made comitted, suffered or done by him the said Joshua Dawson or his Heires, or any other Person or Persons whatsoever claiming or to claime, by from or Under him them or any of them, or the said Henry Temple the said Sir John Temple deceased or the said Hugh Price, and further the said Joshua Dawson and his Heires shall and will from time to time and at all times hereafter on the request and at proper costs and charges in the law of the said Lord Mayor, Sheriffes, Comons and Citizens of the said City of Dublin and their Successors do make perfect, levy, execute and suffer, or cause and procure to be made done, perfected, levyed, executed, and suffered all such further and other lawfull and reasonable act or acts, Deed or Deeds Devices, Conveyances Assurances in the law whatsoever, for the further and better assureing and suremaking and confirming the said hereby granted and released Premises, with their and every of their appurtenances unto the said Lord Mayor, Sheriffes, Comons and Citizens of the said City of Dublin, and their Successors, according to the Tenor and true meaning of these presents, Be it by one or more fine or fines Sur Cognizance de droit come ceo, with Proclamation wherein Anne Wife of the said Joshua Dawson shall joyne if required, Recovery or Recoverys, Release, Confirmation or any other matter or fact, or Record, or both, as by the said Lord Mayor, Sheriffes, Comons and Citizens or their Successors, or their Council learned in the law shall be reasonably advised or devised and required, so as much further Assurances contain no further or other Covenants or Warrants than are herein contained. And that the said Joshua Dawson his heires or Assigns shall and will at all times hereafter produced, or cause to be produced and shewed the said recited Deeds of fee foroms and all other deed or deeds for making out at Title to the said hereby granted and released Premises on any Tryal at Law, or in Equity that shall be commenced for the defence of the Premises, or whensoever it shall be necessary to make out a Title to the same, and the said Joshua Dawson and his Heires the said hereby granted and released Premises with the appurtenances and every part thereof unto the said Lord Mayor, Sheriffes Comons and Citizens and their Successors against him the said Joshua Dawson and his Heires, and the said Henry Temple his Heires and Assignes, and all other Person and Persons whatsoever claiming or to claime by from or under them or either of them, or the said Sir John Temple deceased, or the said Hugh Price or any Person claiming by from or under him, them or any of them, subject to the payment of the said Sugar Loaf Yearly if demanded, shall and will Warrant, and by these presents for ever defend. In Witness whereof the said Joshua Dawson hath here unto put his hand and Seale the day and Yeare of first above written.

J. Dawson

A List of the Goods and Furniture sold by Joshua Dawson Esqre to the Right honourable the Lord Mayor, Sheriffes, Comons and Citizens of the City of Dublin, and to be left in the dwelling house sold to Them.

- Twenty four Brass Locks
- Six Marble Chimney pieces
- The Tapistry Hangings, Silk Window Curtains and Window Seats, and Chimney Glass in the great Bed Chamber
- The Guilt Leather Hangings, four paire of Scarlet Calamanco Window Curtains and Chimney Glass in the Walnut Parlour
- The Indian Callicoe Window Curtains and Seats and Chimney Glass in – the Dantzick Oak Parlour
- The window Curtains and Chimney Glass in the large eating Roome

Title Deeds Glossary

Acquit	Declare someone not guilty of crime or misdemeandour
Alien	Transfer to new ownership
Annuity	Yearly rent, payment for years, life or perpetuity
Appurtenance	Accessory associated with particular activity
Arrears	Debts/payments outstanding and due
Assurance	Positive declaration intended to give confidence
Assure	Secure future payments of an amount with insurance
Behoofe of	Advantage/profit of
Calamanco	Glossy woollen cloth chequered on one side only
Calico	Plain white/unbleached cotton cloth
Commons	Common people regarded as part of political system
Covenant	Formal agreement to pay
Conveyance	Title transfer to property; bargain, sale, lease, release
Deed	Legal document regarding property ownership
Distrain	Seize property or chattels in lieu of rent/money owed
Dower	Interest of a widow in deceased husband's freehold lands
Equity	Law branch (alongside common law concerning fairness)
Esquire	Polite title appended to male surname
Exonerate	Absolve officially from blame
Extent	Size/scale of something
Forom (Forum)	Court/tribunal
Gale	Parcel; land leased to a Freeholder
Hindrance	Obstruction/snag, impediment
Incumbrance (Encumbrance)	Mortgage or other claim on property or assets
Indemnify	Secure against legal responsibility for their actions
Indenture	Legal agreement/contract
Intailes (Entail)	Restrict descent of estate to designated line of heirs
Levy	Seize (property) items to satisfy legal judgement
Liable	Legally answerable/responsible by law
Lot	An assigned/apportioned share
Mearing	Forming a boundary/mere (lake/pond)
Mesne	Legal term for intermediate, middle, between
Messuage	House without buildings or land
Perch	Land area equal to measure of 160th of acre
Procure	Persuade/cause to do something/secure
Recognisance	Appear when summoned
Remise	Cancel a debt or a charge

Rood	Land area equal to measure of quarter of acre
Scituate (situate)	Allot a site to, place, locate
Statute	Written law passed by legislative body
Suit (Lawsuit)	Proceedings in a court of equity
Sure make	Confirm/ensure
Sur Cognizance de droit come ceo	Fine re wrongful possession of land where cognizee (plaintiff) alleges wrongful procession of land by cognisor
Tenor	Actual wording of a document (law)
Termor	Landlord for life, or for a period of years
Third	One of three equal parts into which something is divided
Viz.	Namely, in other words
Wainscot	Wood panelling of lower part of wall in room
Yield	To generate (financial return)/deliver result

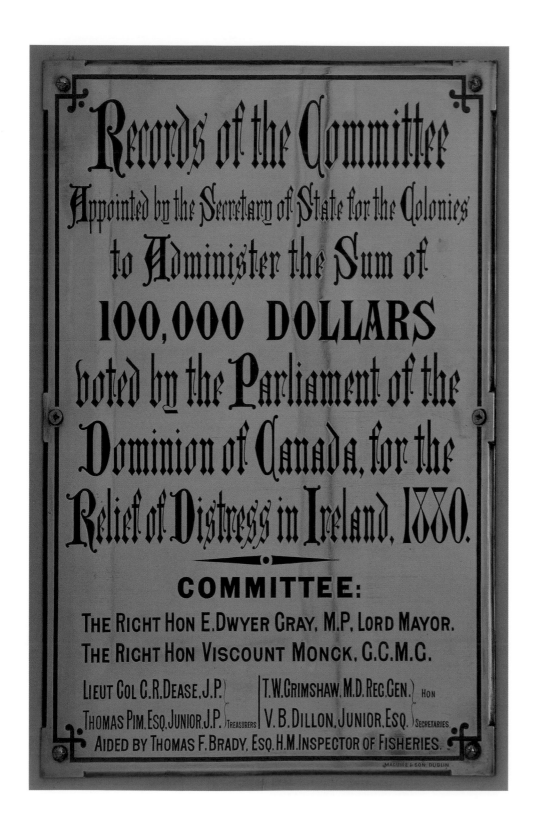

AN GORTA MÓR

TO COMMEMORATE THE GENEROSITY

OF

THE CHOCTAW NATION OF OKLAHOMA

(FORCIBLY REMOVED FROM MISSISSIPPI IN 1831),

WHO, TOGETHER WITH

FIRST NATIONS LOCATED IN UPPER AND LOWER CANADA, RESPONDED WITH IMMENSE KINDNESS AND COMPASSION TOWARDS THE SUFFERING IRISH DURING OUR GREAT FAMINE OF 1847.

THEIR HUMANITY CALLS US TO REMEMBER THE MILLIONS OF HUMAN BEINGS THROUGHOUT OUR WORLD TODAY WHO DIE OF HUNGER AND HUNGER-RELATED ILLNESS IN A WORLD OF PLENTY.

UNVEILED BY THE RT. HON. THE LORD MAYOR, COUNCILLOR DR. SEÁN KENNY, P.C. 29 MAY 1992.

SPONSORED BY: AFrI (ACTION FROM IRELAND) DUBLIN.

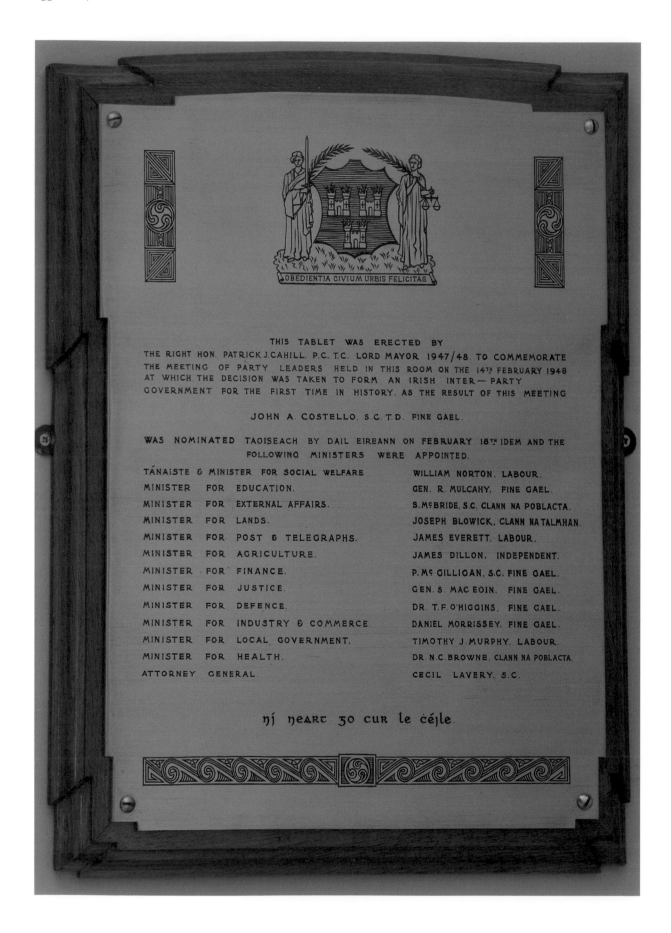

THIS TABLET WAS ERECTED BY
THE RIGHT HON. PATRICK J. CAHILL. P.C. T.C. LORD MAYOR 1947/48. TO COMMEMORATE
THE MEETING OF PARTY LEADERS HELD IN THIS ROOM ON THE 14TH FEBRUARY 1948
AT WHICH THE DECISION WAS TAKEN TO FORM AN IRISH INTER—PARTY
GOVERNMENT FOR THE FIRST TIME IN HISTORY. AS THE RESULT OF THIS MEETING

JOHN A. COSTELLO. S.C. T.D. FINE GAEL.

WAS NOMINATED TAOISEACH BY DAIL EIREANN ON FEBRUARY 18TH IDEM AND THE
FOLLOWING MINISTERS WERE APPOINTED.

TÁNAISTE & MINISTER FOR SOCIAL WELFARE	WILLIAM NORTON, LABOUR.
MINISTER FOR EDUCATION.	GEN. R. MULCAHY, FINE GAEL.
MINISTER FOR EXTERNAL AFFAIRS.	S. McBRIDE, S.C. CLANN NA POBLACTA.
MINISTER FOR LANDS.	JOSEPH BLOWICK, CLANN NA TALMHAN.
MINISTER FOR POST & TELEGRAPHS.	JAMES EVERETT, LABOUR.
MINISTER FOR AGRICULTURE.	JAMES DILLON, INDEPENDENT.
MINISTER FOR FINANCE.	P. McGILLIGAN, S.C. FINE GAEL.
MINISTER FOR JUSTICE.	GEN. S. MAC EOIN. FINE GAEL.
MINISTER FOR DEFENCE.	DR. T.F. O'HIGGINS, FINE GAEL.
MINISTER FOR INDUSTRY & COMMERCE.	DANIEL MORRISSEY. FINE GAEL.
MINISTER FOR LOCAL GOVERNMENT.	TIMOTHY J. MURPHY. LABOUR.
MINISTER FOR HEALTH.	DR. N.C. BROWNE, CLANN NA POBLACTA.
ATTORNEY GENERAL.	CECIL LAVERY, S.C.

ní neart go cur le céile.

Records
of the
Mansion House Committee
1880.
Through which £181,665,9,1 was collected
and distributed for the
Relief of Distress
in Ireland.
during that year.
The Rt honble E. Dwyer Gray. M.P.
lord Mayor Chairman.
TREASURERS.

The Chairman	Alderman hugh Tarpey.
his Grace The Most Revd. Trench.	John Barrington. knt. d.l.
James W. Mackey. knt. d.l.	ex lord Mayor.
high Sheriff.	Jonathan Pim.
William lane Joynt. d.l.	

HON SECRETARIES.

R.W. Bagot. Canon. lld.	T. Maxwell hutton.
James daniel. P.P.	Charles Kennedy.
P. Mc Cabe Fay.	George D. Owens. knt.
V. B. dillon. Jun.	

PLACED IN THE MANSION HOUSE BY PERMISSION OF THE CORPORATION BY RESOLUTION OF DEC. 6TH 1880

MAGUIRE & SON DUBLIN

Records
of the
Mansion House Committee
1880.

Through which **£181.665:9:1.** was collected
and distributed for the

Relief of Distress
in Ireland.
during that year.

The Rt. Honble. E. Dwyer Gray, M.P.
Lord Mayor Chairman.

Treasurers.

The Chairman	Alderman Hugh Tarpey
His Grace The Most Revd. Trench	John Barrington, knt. D.L.
James W. Mackey. knt. D.L.	ex Lord Mayor
High Sheriff	Jonathan Pim
William Lane Joynt D.L.	

Hon. Secretaries

R.W. Bagot. Canon LL.D.	T. Maxwell Hutton
James Daniel, P.P.	Charles Kennedy
P. McCabe Fay	George B. Owens, knt.
V.B. Dillon, Jun.	

PLACED IN THE MANSION HOUSE BY PERMISSION OF THE CORPORATION BY RESOLUTION OF DEC 6TH 1880

MAGUIRE & SON DUBLIN

Records of the
Irish National Exhibition
Erected at a cost of nearly **£20,000.**
in the
Rotunda Gardens, Dublin
by the
Irish Exhibition Company (Limited)
opened
15th August 1882
by the
Right Honourable Charles Dawson, M.P.
Lord Mayor
Chairman of the Company

Directors

E.Dwyer Gray, M.P. High Sheriff	Joseph M. Meade, J.P.
Edward M. Hodgson	Alderman William Meagher
Edward J. Kennedy	William M. Murphy, C.E.
Alderman Michael Kernan	Samuel Smalldridge
James F. Lombard, J.P.	Alfred Webb, T.C.
Timothy Mahony, J.P.	James Winstanley, T.C.
Engineer	Architect
Arthur Dudgeon, C.E.	George C. Ashlin, A.R.H.A.
Solicitors	Auditors
V.B. Dillon & Co.	Kevans & Kean
Secretary	John C. Rooney

J. FAGAN, DUBLIN

Records of the Committee

Appointed by the Secretary of State for the Colonies

to Administer the Sum of

100,000 DOLLARS

voted by the Parliament of the

Dominion of Canada, for the

Relief of Distress in Ireland, 1880.

————:————

COMMITTEE :

THE RIGHT HON E.DWYER GRAY, M.P. LORD MAYOR
THE RIGHT HON VISCOUNT MONCK, G.C.M.G.

LIEUT COL C.R. DEASE, J.P. }	T.W. GRIMSHAW, M.D., REG. GEN.} HON.
THOMAS PIM, ESQ, JUNIOR, J.P. } TREASURERS	V.B. DILLON, JUNIOR, ESQ. } SECRETARIES

AIDED BY THOMAS F. BRADY, ESQ. H.M. INSPECTOR OF FISHERIES

MAGUIRE & SON DUBLIN

An Gorta Mór

To Commemorate the Generosity

of

The Choctaw Nation of Oklahoma

(forcibly removed from Mississippi in 1831)

who, together with

First Nations located in Upper
and Lower Canada, responded

with immense Kindness and Compassion
Towards the Suffering Irish during our

Great Famine of 1847.

Their Humanity calls us to Remember the
millions of human beings throughout our world
today who die of hunger and hunger-related
illness in a world of plenty.

Unveiled by The Rt. Hon, The Lord Mayor,
Councillor Dr. Sean Kenny, P.C. 29 May 1992

Sponsored by : AFrL (Action from Ireland) Dublin

THIS TABLET WAS ERECTED BY
THE RIGHT HON. PATRICK J. CAHILL P.C. T.C. LORD MAYOR 1947/48 TO COMMEMORATE
THE MEETING OF PARTY LEADERS HELD IN THIS ROOM ON THE 14TH FEBRUARY 1948
AT WHICH THE DECISION WAS TAKEN TO FORM AN IRISH INTER-PARTY
GOVERNMENT FOR THE FIRST TIME IN HISTORY. AS THE RESULT OF THIS MEETING

JOHN A. COSTELLO S.C. T.D. FINE GAEL

WAS NOMINATED TAOISEACH BY DAIL EIREANN ON FEBRUARY 18th IDEM AND THE
FOLLOWING MINISTERS WERE APPOINTED

TANAISTE & MINISTER FOR SOCIAL WELFARE	WILLIAM NORTON, LABOUR
MINISTER FOR EDUCATION	GEN. R. MULCAHY, FINE GAEL
MINISTER FOR EXTERNAL AFFAIRS	S. McBRIDE, S.C. CLANN NA POBLACTA
MINISTER FOR LANDS	JOSEPH BLOWICK CLANN NA TALMHAN
MINISTER FOR POST & TELEGRAPHS	JAMES EVERETT, LABOUR
MINISTER FOR AGRICULTURE	JAMES DILLON, INDEPENDENT
MINISTER FOR FINANCE	P. Mc GILLIGAN S.C. FINE GAEL
MINISTER FOR JUSTICE	GEN. S. MAC EOIN, FINE GAEL
MINISTER FOR DEFENCE	DR. T.F. O'HIGGINS, FINE GAEL
MINISTER FOR INDUSTRY & COMMERCE	DANIEL MORRISSEY, FINE GAEL
MINISTER FOR LOCAL GOVERNMENT	TIMOTHY J. MURPHY, LABOUR
MINISTER FOR HEALTH	DR. N.C. BROWNE, CLANN NA POBLACTA
ATTORNEY GENERAL	CECIL LAVERY, S.C.

Ní neart go cur le céile

AUTHORS

Mary Clark is the Dublin City Archivist. She was a member of the inaugural National Archives Advisory Council; honorary secretary of the Irish Society for Archives and a member of the steering group for the local archives survey conducted by the Department of the Environment. She has published widely on the history of Dublin and was editor, along with Alastair Smeaton, of *The Georgian Squares of Dublin*, published by Dublin City Council in 2006. She has also worked on several exhibitions, including *The Story of the Capital* at Dublin's City Hall and *A Vision of the City: Dublin and the Wide Streets Commissioners* with Niall McCullough. She was awarded a doctorate in the History of Art by University College Dublin for her thesis on the Dublin Civic Portrait Collection, which was supervised by Dr. Christine Casey. She is currently series editor, with Máire Kennedy, of Dublin City Council's publications to mark the Decade of Commemorations.

Fanchea Gibson is the current Manager of the Mansion House. A native of Wexford, she previously worked in Dún Laoghaire Corporation and Dún Laoghaire-Rathdown County Council before moving to Dublin City Council in 2008. She was based in the Communications Section producing corporate publications including the Dublin City Council Annual Report before moving to the Mansion House in May 2010. She currently oversees the management of the Office of the Lord Mayor and the upkeep of the Mansion House and has worked with six Lord Mayors to date. Recent projects include the revival of the Lord Mayor's Ball as a charitable venture, and making arrangements for the conferring of the Honorary Freedom of Dublin in 2014 and 2015. She feels privileged to be working in this historic building during its tercentenary celebrations.

Christian Keegan is based in Dublin City Library and Archive, where he works in the Reading Room, and has special responsibility for the production of historic documentation relating to planning in Dublin City. Recent projects include the preparation of an index to the minutes of Dublin City Council, 1881–1987 and the digitisation of the Wide Street Commissions (WSC) collection, Jacobs' Factory collection and the Royal Dublin Fusiliers Association (RDFA) collection. He is currently working on a complementary index to the Dublin Corporation Reports, 1869–1987 and to the minutes of Dublin City Council manuscripts, 1841–1880. He holds a degree (B.A. Hons.) in modern languages from the University of Nottingham, with special reference to German, Russian and Serbo-Croatian, and also holds a library qualification from Aberystwyth University.

Úna Loftus was born in Cootehill, County Cavan and lived most of her life in Clontarf, Dublin. She trained in Home Economics at Sion Hill and taught at Notre Dame Des Missions, Churchtown and Scoil Chaitriona in Churchtown. A fluent Irish speaker, Úna was involved in promoting the Irish language and culture. On moving to Clontarf she co-founded Pobal Cluain Tarbh and from 1960 until her death she was an active member of the committee of Oireachtas na Gaeilge. She spent two terms of three years each as Chairperson and in 2011 was elected to be Uachtarán Oireachtas na Gaeilge. She was the wife of Seán Dublin Bay Loftus (now deceased) and was Lady Mayoress in July 1995 to July 1996. Úna thoroughly enjoyed this role and was an excellent hostess at events in the Mansion House. Her love of Irish history led to her giving tours of the House in both English and Irish up until her death. Úna had a lifelong commitment to community activism and in supporting local democracy. She was a member of the Executive Council of the Community Forum on the Dublin City Development Board from 2000 onwards and was Chairperson from 2009 to 2012. Úna died after a short illness in April 2014.

Nicola Matthews is architectural Conservation Officer for Dublin City Council, with input to the development of planning policy and control, coupled with good conservation practice. She trained at the Dublin Institute of Technology, Bolton Street and subsequently at University College Dublin, where her specialist topic for the Master's in Urban and Building Conservation was based on the construction of Georgian Dublin, focusing on the chronological development of Merrion Square. Her projects outside Dublin include the architectural survey of county Kilkenny for the National Inventory of Architectural Heritage and the assessment of Kildare's historic farmhouses to produce guidelines for their conservation, along with their outbuildings, on behalf of Kildare County Council in partnership with the Heritage Council.

The late **Andrew O'Brien** was the doyen of the Reading Room at Dublin City Library & Archive from 2003 until his untimely death ten years later. He generously shared his encyclopaedic knowledge with researchers, coming up with new avenues which they might explore, and was particularly well-informed about military and maritime history. He was a noted admirer of Admiral Lord Nelson and spoke about Nelson's Pillar many times on radio and television. He had a soft spot for Thomas Dudley, better known as the Dublin character 'Bang-Bang' and recounted tales of his exploits for a television documentary. Andrew is sadly missed by all in the Reading Room.

Susan Roundtree is an RIAI Accredited Grade 1 Conservation Architect. A graduate of DIT, UCD and TCD, she has worked as an architect in private and public practice since 1977. Her work with Dublin City Council (1987–2014) has included, in recent years, conservation and repair works to key historic buildings in civic ownership including the Mansion House. Her published research includes an architectural history of Mountpleasant Square in *The Georgian Squares of Dublin*, 2006 and a history of the use of brick in eighteenth-century Dublin in *The Eighteenth-Century Dublin Town House*, 2010. Her book on local history *Ranelagh in Pictures – a Place in History* was published in 2009.

Patricia Wrafter is an architect with Dublin City Council and is currently working on the interiors of 18th century civic buildings for the City Council. In 2008, Patricia was winner of the Rachel McRory prize in for her Masters in Urban and Building Conservation Thesis 'The influence of Chinoiserie on Irish architecture in the 18th century'. She has

lectured on the Influence of the Orient on Irish architecture and furniture. She is currently researching into Neoclassical Chinoiserie, a previously unrecognised style of architecture first developed by Sir William Chambers and first evident in his work at the Casino at Marino and Charlemont house, Dublin and later at Somerset House in London, for University College London. On this topic, she recently lectured in the Casino at Marino, Dublin for The Office of Public Works in Ireland. As part of her work, Patricia has carried out research in London, Paris and Ireland on oriental carpet design and in particular the history of carpet design in Dublin Castle which has influenced the selection and design of new carpets for the Mansion House.

BIBLIOGRAPHY

Casey, Christine (Ed), *Dublin*, The Buildings of Ireland Series, (Yale, 2005)

Clark, Mary and Hardiman, Nodlaig. *Dublin City Treasures.* (Dublin 1990)

Clark, Mary, 'The Mansion House, Dublin', *Dublin Historic Record*, Vol. LX, No. 2 (2007)

Clark, Mary. *The Dublin Civic Portrait Collection: Patronage, Politics and Patriotism* (forthcoming, 2015)

Baillie Fellow, W, 'Watch and Clockmakers of the World', *Georgian Society Records*, Vol. IV, 1912

Gibney, Arthur. Studies in Eighteenth-Century Building History, unpub PhD thesis, TCD, 1997

Knight of Glin. *Irish Furniture* (Dublin, 2007)

McCabe, Desmond. *St Stephen's Green: Dublin 1660–1875* (Dublin, 2011)

McCullough, Niall. *Dublin an Urban History* (2nd edition, Dublin, 2007)

McEvansoneya, Philip. 'The State Coach of the Lord Mayor of Dublin' *Irish Arts Review* (Yearbook, vol. 17, 2001)

McManus, Ruth & Griffith, Lisa-Marie (eds). *Leaders of the City 1500-1950* (Dublin, 2013)

Usher, Robin, *Dawson Street, Molesworth Street and Kildare Street* (Dublin, 2008)

ACKNOWLEDGEMENTS

The Authors wish to acknowledge the assistance of the staff of Dublin City Library & Archive, the Irish Architectural Archive and the National Library of Ireland who have made us welcome during our research. We are also grateful to Dublin City Council Surveying & Mapping Section and Law Department; Terry Coleman (late of Douglas Interiors); Paul Johnston (late of Johnston Antiques); Dr Edward McParland (architectural historian, TCD); Dr David Griffin (IAA) - inventory notes and visits; Peter Linden; James Adams; Charles Lyons (MUBC historic roofs); Sven Habermann (Conservation Letterfrack); Sean Murphy (Hayes Higgins Partnership); Mary McGrath (paint analysis); Christopher Moore (advisory – Dining Room); Peter Clarke (DIT); Gordon Knaggs (timber consultant); Dr Patricia McCarthy (historic interiors and inventories); Dr Freddie O'Dwyer (architectural historian and advisor DAHG); Finola Reid (Historic Gardens Consultant). Our three photographers, Conor McCabe, Alastair Smeaton and Joanna Travers, have produced excellent images to enhance the book.

This book would not have been possible without the enthusiastic commitment of the staff of the Mansion House. We are particularly grateful to Vincent Norton, Executive Manager, Dublin City Council's Chief Executive Office, for actively facilitating the publication of this book and the purchase of the Joshua Dawson Cup.

It has been a pleasure and a privilege to work on this book to mark the tercentenary of Dublin's Mansion House.

ENDNOTES

The Mansion House, Dublin: a brief history

1   Christine Casey, *The Buildings of Dublin*, (New Haven and London, 2005), p. 504.

2   Mark Girouard, *The English Town: a History of Urban Life* (Yale University Press, 1990), p. 28; T. Oliver, *A New Picture of Newcastle-upon-Tyne* (Newcastle-upon-Tyne, 1831), pp 55-6; Richard Simms, *The Historic Mansion House of Newcastle-upon-Tyne* (Newcastle, 2003). The present Mansion House at Newcastle is the city's third one, which celebrated its golden jubilee in December 2003.

3   John Ingamells, 'The State Room portraits in York Mansion House' in *The Connoisseur* (February 1971).

4   Brian Barber, 'Doncaster Mansion House: an Anniversary Tour' in Brian Elliott (ed.) *Aspects of Doncaster: Discovering Local History*, vol. 2, (Barnsley, 1999), pp 53-68.

5   Sally Jeffrey, *The Mansion House* (London, 1993), p. 18. Also 'Description of the City of Dublin, 1732 by a Citizen of London' where it is noted: "In Dublin is a palace the Lord Mayors keep their Mayoralty in, which piece of grandeur seems to be so well approved by my fellow-citizens of London, as has induced them to believe it may be for the honour of the citizens of London, [that] the chief magistrate should appear in the utmost splendour, therefore at this time a fund is settling to build a palace for the Lord Mayor of London." Reprinted in *Anc. Rec. Dublin*, X p. 528.

6   For an account of some of these early mayoral residences, see Jeffrey, *The Mansion House*, pp 17-19. From the late 17th century, London's Lord Mayors lived in a house at Groveland Court, off Bow Lane, which had been constructed following the Great Fire. When the London Mansion House was commissioned in 1738, this house was sold to Robert Williamson, who turned it into a hotel. The Lord Mayors continued to lodge there until the Mansion House was ready for occupation in 1752. Williamson's Hotel was demolished during the 1930s and was replaced by a tavern; however, a pair of wrought-iron gates presented by William III and Mary II for the original Mayoral residence is still on the site. Ted Bruning, *Historic Pubs of London* (London, 1998), pp 94-5.

7   As at Newcastle-upon-Tyne, the present Mansion House at Bristol is the third one.

8   Sir John T. and Lady Gilbert (eds) *Calendar of Ancient Records of Dublin*, 19 vols. (Dublin, 1889–1944), vol. II p. viii. (Henceforth *Anc. Rec. Dublin*)

9   *Anc. Rec. Dublin* I p. 484

10   Ibid., I, p. 449

11   John Derricke, *The Image of Ireland* (London, 1581). The event is captured in an engraving dated 1581 but a caption praises Sidney's 'triple renown' – a reference to his three campaigns against Irish forces, of which the last was in summer 1569, when Walter Eustace was Mayor of Dublin.

12   Ibid., II, pp 329.

13   Ibid., I p. 38.

14   Ibid., I pp 42-56.

15   John T. Gilbert, *History of the City of Dublin* (Dublin, 1854–59), vol. I, p. 15; F.J. Holden 'Property taxes in Old Dublin' in *Dublin Historical Record*, vol. XIII, pp 133-7; Claude Blair and Ida Delamer, 'The Dublin Civic Swords' in *Proceedings of the Royal Irish Academy*, vol. 88, C, no. 5 (1988).w

16   *Anc. Rec. Dublin.*, VI, pp 276-7.

17   Ibid., VI, pp xii-xiii. Bell was a presbyterian merchant who lived on Ormond Quay.

18   Ibid., VI, p 489.

19   Ibid., VI, pp 472-3.

20   John Allen was a colonel in the Williamite army and was an M.P. for Co. Dublin. He held property in Stillorgan and Dalkey, Co. Dublin and also in Co. Wicklow.

21   R.B. McDowell, *Land & Learning: Two Irish Clubs* (Dublin, 1993), p. 122.

22   *Anc. Rec. Dublin* VI, p. 487.

23   Turtle Bunbury in *Irish Daily Mail*, 1 May 2015.

24   Public Record Office of Northern Ireland, D.618/235 Genealogy of the Dawson Family.

25   I am indebted to Dr. Raymond Refaussé for this information.

26   In 1991, a small street on the west side of Dawson Street, which gives access to the Royal Irish Automobile Club, was named Joshua Lane by Dublin City Council, as a further tribute to the person who had done so much to develop the area. The distinctive spelling of

St. Ann's Church and Parish was chosen in tribute to Dawson's wife Ann (rather than Queen Anne); I am indebted to Rev. Dudley Levistone Cooney for this information.

27   *Anc. Rec. Dublin*, VI, pp 534-7.

28   Ibid., VI, pp 534-7.

29   There is no evidence that the sugar-loaf was ever demanded or supplied.

30   *Anc. Rec. Dublin*, VI, 535.

31   Dublin City Library & Archive, Deeds to the City, No. 13.

32   A chimney glass was a mirror which was positioned on a chimney breast, typically over a fireplace.

33   Dublin City Library & Archive, Deeds to the City No. 13

34   *Anc. Rec. Dublin*, VI, pp 544-5.

35   Ibid., VII, p. 16. Sadly this inventory has not survived.

36   The civic year began and ended at Michaelmas, 29 September.

37   John Lodge and Mervyn Archdall, *The Peerage of Ireland* (Dublin, 1789), p. 213. Francis Stoyte died without issue and left his fortune to his brother John Stoyte. The name descended down the family and later John Stoytes were variously a landowner in the village of Streete, Co. Westmeath; a silversmith in Dublin; and an architect who designed Stoyte House in Maynooth, Co. Kildare.

38   The Riding of the Franchises was a perambulation of the Dublin city boundaries on horseback, led by the Lord Mayor, which took place once every three years.

39   Charles Brooking's map was issued in a number of editions. An example of the first edition is on display in the Royal Irish Academy and an example of the second edition is held with the Dublin Civic Museum collections. A modern edition, based on reproductions of the R.I.A. and Civic Museum maps, was published by the Irish Architectural Archive in 1983, with an introduction by Maurice Craig.

40   Originally called Dawson's Bridge, this small village assumed its present name around 1710 when Dawson began to re-design it. Samuel Lewis, *A Topographical Dictionary of Ireland* (London, 1837), vol. I, pp 294-5.

41 *Anc. Rec. Dublin*, IX, p. 97.

42 The Dalys were the most powerful family in Galway during the mid-18th century. Charles Daly was Mayor of Galway in 1762 and James Daly was Mayor three years later; the family also held the parliamentary seat. See James Kelly, 'The Politics of Protestant Ascendancy: County Galway 1650–1832' in Gerard Moran and Raymond Gillespie (eds), *Galway: History & Society* (Dublin, 1996), pp 229-270.

43 Sovereign House in Kinsale, which was built in 1706, was the private residence of two of the town's first citizens, Antony Stawell and William Newman. Sovereign's House, The Mall, Armagh, was built in 1810 for Arthur Kelly, who was first citizen of Armagh almost continuously from 1805 until 1837. C.E.B. Brett, *Buildings of County Armagh* (Belfast, 1999), entry no. 118. Neither building was an official mayoral residence. In Belfast it is customary for an ornate lamp-standard, garnished with the city arms, to be placed outside the private residence of the current Lord Mayor. A bedroom with wash-stand, identical to a first-class cabin on the *Titanic* and made by craftsmen from Harland and Wolff at the same time as the ill-fated liner, is provided for the Lord Mayor in Belfast City Hall.

44 From 'Description of the City of Dublin, 1732. By a Citizen of London.' Re-printed in *Anc. Rec. Dublin*, X, p 528.

45 *Anc. Rec. Dublin*, VII, p. xxi.

46 Ibid., XIV, p. 221.

47 Ibid., VII, p. xx.

48 These cups are still owned by Dublin City Council and are on display in the standing exhibition at Dublin's City Hall.

49 Hill, *From Patriots to Unionists*, p. 79.

50 Ibid., pp 82, 99, 392. An anonymous ode, entitled *Astrea's Congratulation*, was published in 1733 to celebrate French's victory in a by-election that year.

51 W.G. Strickland, 'The State Coach of the Lord Mayor of the City of Dublin and the State Coach of the Earl of Clare, Lord Chancellor of Ireland' in *R.S.A.I. Jn*, vol. LI, (1921), pp 49-67 (henceforth Strickland, 'State Coaches').

52 Hill, *From Patriots to Unionists*, pp 83, 109, 114, 117, 391. An anonymous tribute to Cooke for his opposition to the money bill was published in 1754 under the title *The Free Citizens' Address to Sir Samuel Cooke, Bart.*

53 *Anc. Rec. Dublin*, VII, pp 102-3, 114-6.

54 Ibid., X, p. 326.

55 Noreen Casey and David Griffin, 'The Mansion House, Dublin'. Unpublished report commissioned by Dublin Corporation from the Irish Architectural Archive, 1987. Also *Anc. Rec. Dublin*, XI, pp 234, 272-3.

56 Mary Clark, 'A Principal Ornament for the Mayoralty House: a portrait by Joshua Reynolds' in *Irish Arts Review* (Yearbook, 1999), pp 154-6.

57 Private collection; reproduced as fig. 63 in Anne Crookshank and the Knight of Glin, *Ireland's Painters, 1600–1940* (Yale, 2002), p. 48.

58 *Anc. Rec. Dublin*, XIV, pp 276-7.

59 Ibid., XVI, pp 184-8; Dublin City Archives, City Surveyor's Maps, C1/S1/63 and C1/S1/64.

60 *Anc. Rec. Dublin*, XVII, pp 536-8. The shortfall was discovered in the accounts of City Treasurer Alderman John Carleton who resigned in disgrace.

61 Ibid., XVI, pp 376-80.

62 John James McGregor, *New Picture of Dublin*, (Dublin, 1821), p. 164. This book was illustrated with engravings showing Dublin's principal buildings but again the Mansion House was excluded.

63 G.N. Wright, *An Historical Guide to the City of Dublin* (Dublin, 1825), p. 105.

64 Semple's son, also called John, was City Architect from 1829 until 1842 and designed many churches for the Church of Ireland in the late 1820s. See Maurice Craig, 'John Semple and his Churches' in *Irish Arts Review*, (Yearbook, 1989–90), pp 145-50.

65 For an image of this portrait, see Appendix 4.

66 *Anc. Rec. Dublin*, XVIII, p. 113.

67 Dublin City Council minutes, C1/A1/13, pp 221-2; C2/A1/15, pp 83-4.

68 Christine Casey, op. cit. pp 504-5.

69 Henry Shaw, *The Dublin Pictorial Guide and Directory* (Dublin, 1850; re-printed 1988); elevations for Dawson Street.

70 Christine Casey, op. cit. pp 504-5.

71 *Minutes of Dublin City Council*: C1/A1/33

72 *Irish Times*, 2 Jan 1882.

73 Minutes of Dublin City Council: C2/A1/33, pp 312-3; 362-3; 387-8; 467-8.

74 *Irish Times*, 7 February 1872.

75 The archives of the Mansion House Fund for Relief of Distress in Ireland and the Canadian Fund for Relief of Distress in Ireland are both held in Dublin City Library & Archive.

76 Online Concordance to *Ulysses*, Project Gutenberg edition, line 11200, chapter Wandering Rocks (henceforth *Ulysses* Concordance).

77 *Ulysses* Concordance, line 11919, Wandering Rocks.

78 Ibid., line 21468, Circe.

79 Ibid., line 8056, Lestrygonians, 17064, Nausicaa.

80 Ibid.,, line 21448, Circe.

81 www.nationalarchives.ie/census 1901.

82 www.nationalarchives.ie/census 1911.

83 Bureau of Military History, Witness Statement No. 465 (henceforth BMH W.S. 465) Mary O'Sullivan, Secretary to the Lord Mayor of Dublin.

84 Ibid., p. 2.

85 Ibid., p. 2.

86 Ibid., p. 4.

87 Ibid., p. 10.

88 Thomas J. Morrissey, *Patriot and Man of Peace: Laurence O'Neill (1864-1943): Lord Mayor of Dublin 1917-1924* (Dublin City Council, 2014).

89 BMH W.S. 465, p. 11.

90 The British army occupied City Hall from 22 December 1920 until 21 January 1922, when the building was ceded to the newly-established Irish Free State. City Hall was then used as the headquarters of the Irish Provisional Government from 22 January to 23 March 1922 and was subsequently occupied by the Irish Free State army during the Civil War. *Dublin Corporation Printed Reports*, no. 322 of 1923, vol. II, pp 683-6.

91 *Printed Minutes of Dublin City Council*, 1938, items 19, 26.

92 Patrick Abercrombie, Sydney A. Kelly and Manning Robertson, *County Borough of Dublin and Neighbourhood* (Dublin, 1941), pp 37-8

93 For reports of Kathleen Clarke's election as lord mayor, and her refusal to be invested with the chain presented to Dublin by William of Orange, see *Irish Independent*, *Irish Press* and *Irish Times*, 28 June 1939.

94 Kathleen Clarke's action echoes a similar move by Douglas Hyde when he became president of Ireland in 1937 and removed all remaining royal portraits from Arus an Uachtaráin, the former Viceregal Lodge. See Róisín Kennedy, *Dublin Castle Art* (Dublin, 1999), p. 49.

95 DCLA, Manuscript minutes of General Purposes Committee for 10 October 1939, vol. IV, pp 50-1. The portraits of Victoria and William III were stored at the Municipal Gallery while the National Gallery of Ireland provided storage facilities for the portrait of George IV and another picture, wrongly believed to be a portrait of Charles II by Sir Peter Lely (now identified as a portrait of the duke of Buckingham). Meanwhile, the frames to the portraits of Victoria and George IV were stored in the Iveagh Markets.

96 See article by Helen Litton to mark the 60th anniversary of Kathleen Clarke's election as lord mayor, in 'An Irishwoman's Diary' *The Irish Times*, 22 June 1999.

97 *The Irish Times*, 12 August 1939.

98 Smokey went into the Lord Mayor's Garden each morning to mark his territory and when he was finished he sat underneath the Mansion House portico – as there was no cat flap, he had to be patient. Invariably, someone from La Stampa restaurant across the road would phone the Lady Mayoress to say 'Your cat is outside your front door, waiting to get in!' I am indebted to Mrs. Peggy Doyle for this lovely story, which sums up the special quality of life in Dublin's Mansion House.

The Mansion House: Historical and Architectural Context

1 Desmond McCabe, *St Stephen's Green, Dublin, 1660-1875*

2 The spelling of Ann suggesting that the church was dedicated to Dawson's wife and not to Queen Anne.

3 Miles Lewis (ed.) *Elements of Architectural Style - Baroque 1625-1714* (New York, 2008).

4 Hilary Ballon, *The Paris of Henri IV* (New York, 2008), p. 7.

5 Nuala T. Burke, 'An Early Modern Dublin Suburb: The Estate of Francis Aungier, Earl of Longford', in *Irish Geography*, 6:4 (1972), pp 380-5; Robin Usher, 'Domestic architecture, the old city and the suburban challenge, c. 1660 – 1700' in Christine Casey (ed.) *The eighteenth-century Dublin townhouse* (Dublin, 2010) pp 59 – 72.

6 Edward McParland, referencing reports of Deputy Keeper of the Records, Ireland.

7 Mary Clark, 'The Mansion House, Dublin' in *Dublin Historical Record*, Vol. LX, No.2.

8 McCabe, op. cit.; Anne Plumptre, *Narrative of residence in Ireland* (1817), pp 52-3.

9 Semple's roof was replaced in 1999 with the current roof form without dormer windows.

10 In 1752 the equestrian statue of King George I by Van Nost was relocated at the Mansion House following its removal from Essex Bridge. It was put at the rear of the house but moved to the side garden in 1798 and can be seen in the Dawson Street elevation peering over the wall of the garden in Henry Shaw's *Pictorial Directory of Dublin*, 1850. It was removed from public view sometime after the foundation of the new state and eventually purchased and re-erected at the Barber Institute of Fine Art at the University of Birmingham, England.

The Mansion House: An Architectural Survey

1 Queen Anne style describes architecture in the English Baroque style built during the reign of Queen Anne 1702-1714, generally domestic buildings of modest scale with features that include sweeping steps leading to a carved stone door case, rows of painted sash windows in box frames set flush with the outside brickwork, often of the same dimensions on ground and first floors, stone quoins emphasising corners, and typical box-like double pile plans two rooms deep. Examples in England include Buckingham House 1703 which was built as a townhouse but acquired by George III in 1762 and incorporated into what subsequently became Buckingham Palace.

2 Charles Brooking, Dublin, 1728. 'The Lord Mayors House' is just one of the many public buildings illustrated in this extraordinary graphic evocation of Dublin at this time.

3 *Anc. Rec. Dublin*, VI, pp 534-7.

4 The coach house was built for the same coach in use today. The State Coach of the Lord Mayor of Dublin, built by William Whitton, made its first appearance on the streets of the city on 4 Nov 1791 to celebrate the birthday of William III, see Philip McEvansoneya, 'A Colourful Spectacle Restored The State Coach of the Lord Mayor of Dublin', *Irish Arts Review* (Yearbook, 2001), pp 81-7.

5 Simon Vierpyl (c1725-1810) was paid £36.19s.3d for stone work at the Mansion House. He is widely regarded as the finest stone mason for decorative carving in eighteenth-century Dublin who worked at the Royal Exchange, the Blue Coat School and the Casino at Marino.

6 'Tour Through Dublin City' first published in *Walker's Hibernian Magazine*, 1783 and reprinted in part in *Dublin Historical Record*, Vol. XVIII, 1961

7 For example, Molyneux House, Peter Street, Dublin or Red House, Youghal, Co. Cork.

8 'You may conceive what the style of building was here formerly when I tell you that the Mansion House of the Lord Mayor is a brick house of two stories, with windows of but two panes' breadth on each.' Campbell, *Philosophical Survey of the South of Ireland*, (Dublin, 1778), p.24.

9 G. N. Wright, *An Historical Guide to the City of Dublin*, (London, 1821).

10 'A Summer Day in Dublin', in W.M. Thackeray, *The Irish Sketch Book,1842-4* (Oxford, 1863).

11 Ball, Francis, *The History of The County of Dublin*, (Dublin, 1920) pp. 1066-7

12 Hugh Byrne was city architect for Dublin Corporation from 1841-1866.

13 This is the Lord Mayor's official coat of arms, similar to the Dublin City Arms – three castles of Dublin on a shield – but if you look closely there is a hat on top of the shield. This hat is called the Cap of Maintenance and traditionally this was carried in front of the Lord Mayor whenever he walked through the streets of Dublin as a sign to the people that they should uncover their heads in the presence of the first citizen.

14 Illustrated in *The Irish Builder*, 1 March 1896.

15 Mary McGrath, The Mansion House, Report, June 2013 [paint analysis by Catherine Hassell].

16 Gibney, Arthur, 'Studies in Eighteenth-Century Building History', unpublished PhD thesis, TCD, 1997.

17 Susan Roundtree, 'History of Clay Brick as a Building Material in Ireland', unpublished thesis, TCD 1999.

18 Daniel Tracy was assigned to carry out this work, along with slating of other public buildings in the city, at a yearly salary of £20 over a 15-year period. *Anc. Rec. Dublin*, IX, p 97.

19 Recent dendrology research at 9 & 9A Aungier Street (1680s) has confirmed a similar construction method for this C17th date and the use of pine rather than oak for structural beams.

20 *Irish Georgian Society Records*, Vol. IV, 1912, p. 104, notes that the staircase is 'in two flights instead of four, as might have been expected at this period.'

21 Information from Sven Habermann, Conservation Letterfrack, June 2011. The only other staircase of yew we are aware of in Ireland is in Birr Castle, Co. Offaly.

22 *Anc. Rec. Dublin* (add reference)

23 Calamanco is a glazed woolen stuff of Flanders woven with satin twill and checkered in the warp, so that the checks are seen on one side only. Much used in the 18th century.

24 Comments on the fittings and furnishings noted in the 1715 agreement courtesy of Dr Patricia McCarthy.

25 The popular conception of the interior of a Queen Anne house c. 1710 is still of one with pine paneling, or wainscoting, painted

26 Gibney, Arthur, 'Studies in Eighteenth-Century Building History', unpublished PhD thesis, TCD, 1997.

27 *Dublin Corporation Reports*, 1934, Item 451: reconstruction of Oak Room roof £704 by Messrs. J. Keegan and later the same year entire reconstruction of room £2,400.

28 Mary McGrath, 'The Mansion House', report September 2012 [paint analysis by Catherine Hassell]

29 *Anc. Rec. Dublin*, XI, p.154.

30 *Anc. Rec. Dublin*, XI, pp 272-3.

31 *Dublin Builder*, 15 Dec 1864, p.261.

32 *Irish Times*, 10 Mar 1900; *Irish Builder* 42, 1 Apr 1900, p.323.

33 *Dublin Corporation Reports*, 1899, no. 213 records the issuing of a contract to Messrs, Sibthorpe in the sum of £390 in reponse to a specification drawn up by the City Architect for the 'thorough renovation' of the Mansion House. The firm of 'Henry Sibthorpe & Son' traded under this name for about a century and a half until it eventually closed in the 1970s. After the firm closed, the contents of the office were thrown out. Much of this material was rescued from a skip. Some of the drawings which were retrieved are in the Irish Architectural Archive; there are also some photographs of the firm's work. Written material from the same source - correspondence, letter books, ledgers, receipts and other documents - dating from 1823 to 1963 is in the National Archives. The company was based just around the corner from the Mansion House at 33 Molesworth Street from the 1880s.

34 The plan, we believe, was prepared as part of a survey of City Estate properties sometime after 1885.

35 These bedrooms were created in 1932 to accommodate the Papal Legate to the Eucharistic Congress, Cardinal Lauri, and his entourage.

36 *Dublin Corporation Reports* 1934, Item 451.

37 Irish Architectural Archive, online Dictionary of Irish Architects 1720-1940, Hay, Mountiford John, Dublin builder admitted a freeman of the City of Dublin in 1798, elected a sheriff in 1803. Hay was responsible for erecting the new circular room at the Mansion House for the reception of George IV in 1821. The Corporation passed a resolution in that year that he be allowed the sum of three hundred guineas as compensation in full for his great activity and extraordinary exertions in erecting and completing the King's Room at the Mansion House in the very limited time allowed for the same. On 10 July 1822 and again on 17 October 1822 the Mansion House Committee of Dublin Corporation recommended the payment of twelve guineas to Hay for work done at the Sheriffs Room. In 1835 he was paid for rebuilding the Mansion House chimneys.

38 Semple's roof was replaced in 1999 with the current roof form without dormer windows.

39 Dr Anthony Meyler, 9 Dawson Street, published a book, *Observations on Ventilation*, sometime before 1822. The book was the substance of lectures, delivered on this subject, at the request of the Dublin Society, in their theatre, in 1818.

40 *The Irish Builder*, 13 Jan 1855, p.17.

41 These windows were removed in the 1990s remodelling of the roof and are in storage.

42 *The Irish Builder*, 25 June 1892, p.510.

43 *The Irish Builder*, 1 Apr 1900, p.323.

44 *Reports and Printed Documents of the Corporation of Dublin*, 1884, Vol.2, pp. 1-2.

45 Ibid.,1891, Vol.1, pp. 41-2.

46 *Freemans Journal*, 7 Feb 1894, p.6. & 20 Feb 1894, p.6.

47 *Freemans Journal*, 1 Mar 1892, p.6.

48 IAA, Dictionary of Irish Architects, Ashlin, George Coppinger, 1837-1921.

49 The design was developed as a collaborative process between Dublin City Council, Sean Harrington Architects and Shaffrey Associates with Finola Reid as the historic garden consultant.

50 Patsy Mitchell in conversation with Mary Clark, City Archivist, in 2002.

Appendix 4: Catalogue of furniture in the Mansion House

1 George Walker, (Dublin 1774-1795 active). Watch and Clockmakers of the world, vol 1. by William Baillie Fellow of the institute of physics N.A.G. Press Ltd London.

2 Furnishing of room as per James Adam catalogue, May 2008.

3 Sven Habermann, Manager Conservation Letterfrack, Co. Galway, Ireland.

4 *Furnishing of room as per Adams catalogue of May 2008 to be revised by Johnston Antiques, 2014.*

5 *Paul Johnston, Johnston Antiques, 2014.*

6 According to Paul Johnston, Johnston Antiques.

INDEX

Compiled by Julitta Clancy